FOUNDATION OF ALGORITHMS
IN
C++11

VOLUME 1

USING AND EXTENDING C++11, BOOST AND BEYOND

REVISED EDITION

Algocoders Series

This series focuses on using and extending C++11, Boost and beyond. Books in this series address the practical need of both users and library authors. Initial titles cover foundational aspect of algorithms. Forthcoming works will expand that core. Ultimately the series will cover other evolutionary software systems. The series goal is to enhance your ability to produce, maintain and extend world class software.

Our website is : **http://www.algocoders.com**

Send all comments for this series to :
`paranoids@algocoders.com`

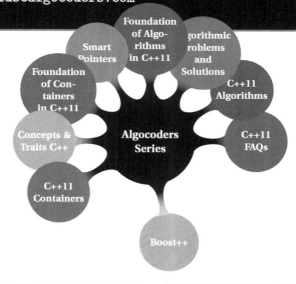

Chandrashekhar Kumar

Aditya Kant Sharma

Foundation of Algorithms in C++11

Volume 1

Algocoders

Breathless Paranoids

Using and Extending C++11, Boost and Beyond

Chandrashekhar Kumar   **Aditya Kant Sharma**

The authors have taken care in the preparation of this book, but make no expressed or implied warranty of any kind and assume no responsibility for errors or omissions. No liability is assumed for incidental or consequential damages in connection with or arising out of the use of the information or programs contained herein.

For more information, visit us on the Web: www.algocoders.com

For comments, mail us at: paranoids@algocoders.com

Foundation of Algorithms in C++11 **Volume 1**

Typesetting of this book is done in LaTeX

ISBN-13: 978-1481965545
ISBN-10: 1481965549

List Of Chapters

i

27 Chapter 3
Sound Interface

Using C++11 Features

33 Chapter 4
Template Aliases

Concept Design

Legacy Codebase

Evolution

List of Programs

*

Preface

This book or booklet is an attempt to voice our understanding of foundation of algorithms newly introduced in C++11 from programmers' perspective who wish to keep themselves abreast with latest advent in C++ and beyond, but quite often than less, find themselves amidst a myriad of disconnecting information, simply due to sheer size of tremendous information available at hands reach, leading to a vast array of tips n techniques. Nonetheless, when it comes to applying same to their day-today problems, they end up struggling a lot to find the apt one.

What happened to us ?

We were going through a similar cycle in a round-a-robin fashion since a long time. We were almost lost in the jungle many-a-times, but fortunately we stumbled across few beacon lights in this process, like in 2009, the most astonishing book we have ever seen was *Elements of Programming* by none other than *Alexander Stepanov et al.*. We played a lot with the available parser written by *Sean Parent* to understand the mathematical underpinnings of the programming logic with our fallible minds. Prior to this, we used to rely on the book *The Science of Programming* by *David Gries* for treatment of foundational aspect of day-today programming.

What were we doing by then ?

Prior to this, we were struggling to understand the C++0x concepts with the help of ConceptGCC, courtesy *Doug Gregor et al.*. But soon after, the July 2009 meeting in Frankfurt, Germany, the C++ Standards Committee voted to remove "concepts" from C++0x, and due to limited time to experiment at our disposal, we decided to let this go out of daily activities. It looked like to us that we had to unlearn more than to learn by then.

Plagued with boost ?

Occasionally, we used to find some solace while looking closely at the internals of boost libraries, especially, BCL(Boost Concept Check), BGL(Boost Graph Libraries), Spirit, Phoenix.

6th August, 2011: Lo! Behold! C++11 standard was out!!
But there was no book around to help us re-understand this new world precisely.

Looking at the presentations and videos at boostcon 2011 and 2012, we decided to start making notes while working with solutions to few of these. Then we never looked back and complained! We realized these notes are going to be of paramount importance, at least for us!! We decided to release these notes as and when it is ready, for people like us, to help learn to a better programmer, but with no strings attached with respect to correctness of the approach herewith.

Approach

This is the very first of this series which is out as promised above! We have adopted a top-down approach to instil our notes in a cohesive manner. The style is pedagogical : we took an algorithm, newly introduced in C++11, looked at its usage, patterns, limitations, corner-cases, preconditions, post-conditions, constraints etc. while keeping a close eye on the interface, its possible evolution in ongoing works like the *Origin C++ Libraries* by *Andrew Sutton*, *Contract++*, *A Concept Design of the STL* by *Bjarne Stroustrup et al.* and other efforts to port boost libraries to C++11 as well as works at libcxx and libstdc++ with focus on C++11. We tried to present a coherent approach to address the needs of programmers like us, who is keenly interested to apply these at work, with little or less risk, without much indulging into the internals of intermediate evolution.

Going forward, we hope to practice and preach knuthian rigor for day-to-day programmer like us!!

Stay Tuned !!!

Have Fun !!!

Chandrashekhar Kumar
Aditya Kant Sharma

Acknowledgement

We dedicate this book to C++ communities who strive to achieve and stay at pinnacle of programming, without compromise to rigor and correctness, how much ever virtual it may look like at any given point of time.

We are especially thankful to Alexander Stepanov, Dijkstra, Gries, Don Knuth, Bjarne Stroustrup, Eric Niebler, Harmut Kaiser and Andrew Sutton, who taught us (still learning) the science of programming by their relentless works(still ongoing!).

Who we are ?

Chandrashekhar Kumar

He holds a degree in Integrated M.Sc.(5 yrs) in Physics from IIT Kanpur. He has been programming in C++ since last 12 years. Currently, he is working with Sapient India Pvt Ltd. He loves to hack gcc, gdb, valgrind, clang, boost, TEX and pours inside the works of Knuth.

Aditya Kant Sharma

He holds a B.Tech. degree from MITS-G. He has been programming in C++ since last 8 years. Currently, he is working with Sapient India Pvt Ltd. He loves to dive inside the internals of C++, Templates hijacking, MFC, STL, Boost, Loki, Design Patterns, LATEX. He is reviving the bandagaon of spearheading ruminations on C++11 and beyond en masse.

Part I

Motivation

Chapter **1**

Kick Off

1.1 std::copy_backward

*L*et us begin our journey in a pragmatic way, so called disciplined way, which is a path of patience, brevity and perseverance. Let us pick a trivial-looking algorithm introduced in C++11, say *std::copy_backward*. Initial focus will be to start using it in order to understand it better with its mere usage. Then try to incrementally validate our understanding garnered so far with some little twisters woven around concepts, traits and beyond.

Kind of *Reductio ad absurdum.*

1.1.1 Interface

Its interface as declared in the header *algorithm* of section 25.3, mutating sequence operations, section 25.3.1 of C++11 Standard, *ISO/IEC 14882:2011(E)*, which looks as follows:

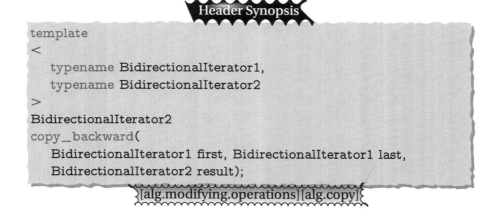

```
template
<
    typename BidirectionalIterator1,
    typename BidirectionalIterator2
>
BidirectionalIterator2
copy_backward(
    BidirectionalIterator1 first, BidirectionalIterator1 last,
    BidirectionalIterator2 result);
```
[alg.modifying.operations][alg.copy]

1.1.2 Description

What will it do ?

☞It copies $[first, last)$ into $[result - (last - first), result)$: iterating in backward direction, i.e.,
starting from $last - 1$ vs $result - 1$ and proceeding to $first$ vs $result - (last - first)$. This is because as we know that $last$ points to one past the end of the source and $result$ points to one past the end of the destination.

Please note that in the expression $result - (last - first)$, both the result and last have that extra one, i.e., so called past the end. However, due to subtraction(courtesy to pointer-like arithmetic) this offset gets subsided, annulled or balanced.

1.2 Uniform Initialization

Let us start using it right away!

In our first example, let the source be a collection of integers, say, $std ::$
$vector < int >$, as follows:

source
```
std::vector<int> v = {1, 2, 3, 4, 5};
```

This nice looking syntax is known as Uniform Initialization which is newly
introduced in C++11.

This means any initialization during the declaration can be done with

☞ parentheses

☞ braces and/or

☞ assignment operators

Here the identifier being declared designates a variable being initialized
by this process of uniform initialization.

The standard[1] summarizes it as :

> *initializer:*
> > *brace-or-equal-initializer*
> > *(expression-list)*
>
> *brace-or-equal-initializer:*
> > *= initializer-clause*
> > *braced-init-list*
>
> *initializer-clause:*
> > *assignment-expression*
> > *braced-init-list*
>
> *initializer-list:*
> > *initializer-clause* . . . $_{opt}$
> > *initializer-list , initializer-clause* . . . $_{opt}$

---
[1]ISO/IEC 14882:2011(E)

braced-init-list:
    { *initializer-list* , $_{opt}$ }
    { }

This means we can also write our tiny vector as follows:

```
std::vector<int> v {1, 2, 3, 4, 5};
```

1.3   copy_backward in Action

Now about the destination where we want to copy the stuff from our vector:

```
std::list<int> l;
```

Let us set the algorithm in action:

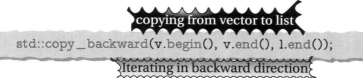

```
std::copy_backward(v.begin(), v.end(), l.end());
```

This compiles fine with clang 3.3:

```
clang version 3.3 (trunk 169585)
Target: x86_64-unknown-linux-gnu
Thread model: posix
```

And it compiles ok with gcc 4.8 too:

```
gcc (GCC) 4.8.0 20121209 (experimental)
Copyright (C) 2012 Free Software Foundation, Inc.
```

But it crashed during execution: Segmentation fault (core dumped): with gcc with the following backtrace:

```
#0  0x00007ffff728c59c in free () from /lib/x86_64-linux-gnu/libc.so.6
#1  0x00000000004016ce in __gnu_cxx::new_allocator<int>::deallocate
(int*, unsigned long) () at
/usr/local/include/c++/4.8.0/ext/new_allocator.h:110
#2  0x000000000040143a in std::_Vector_base<int, std::allocator<int>
>::_M_deallocate(int*, unsigned long) ()
    at /usr/local/include/c++/4.8.0/bits/stl_vector.h:175
#3  0x0000000000401109 in std::_Vector_base<int, std::allocator<int>
>::~_Vector_base() () at
/usr/local/include/c++/4.8.0/bits/stl_vector.h:161
#4  0x0000000000400ea1 in
std::vector<int, std::allocator<int> >::~vector() ()
    at /usr/local/include/c++/4.8.0/bits/stl_vector.h:417
#5  0x0000000000400c7f in main () at copy_backward_1_v2.cpp:13
```

So, there was indeed some problem with the above usage of copy_backward. We plan to return back to the details of this crash sometime later in this book.

1.4   range-based for statement

Then we tried printing the contents of the destination list, expecting it to be filled up with the contents of the vector:

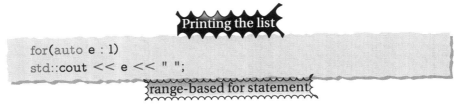

Printing the list

```
for(auto e : l)
  std::cout << e << " ";
```

range-based for statement

This is known as range-based for statement [2], another new language feature in C++11, which can be depicted something like the following :

---

[2]Please refer our website www.algocoders.com for more details about this topic in the forthcoming book *C++11 FAQs*

range-based for statement

```
{
    auto && __range = range-init;
    for (auto __begin = begin-expr,
              __end = end-expr;
              __begin != __end;
              ++__begin
        )
    {
        for-range-declaration = *__begin;
        statement
    }
}
```

internal implementation strategy

And it was not that difficult to figure out that there will be no output when we try to print the list.

1.5 Implicit Precondition

In order to understand it better, we tried printing the size of the list with :

```
std::cout << l.size() << std::endl;
```

And the size obtained was 0.

We realized that this algorithm doesn't create space or insert into the destination, but simply copies, as was implicit in its naively looking interface.

So we learned that:

The destination should be large enough to accommodate source.

1.5.1 Meeting Precondition

Let us set the destination to be of the same size as that of the source vector:

destination with enough space

```
std::list<int> l(v.size()); // enough space
```

Then after running the algorithm, it prints the contents of the list as :
`1 2 3 4 5`

1.6 Verification

We thought of verifying the algorithm as follows:

verification!

The contents of v should be equal to that of l

```
assert(std::equal(v.begin(), v.end(), l.begin()));
```

1.7 Readable Interface

As an astute reader, you must have noticed that we passed *list.end()* as
the third argument to the *copy_backward*, so we would like to read the
interface as follows:

renaming third parameter

```
template
<
    typename BidirectionalIterator1,
    typename BidirectionalIterator2
>
BidirectionalIterator2 copy_backward(
BidirectionalIterator1 source_start,
BidirectionalIterator1 source_end,
BidirectionalIterator2 destination_end)
```

1.8   More Usage

What if we want to copy the first 2 elements of the vector to its end?

> **source and destination is in the same sequence**
> ```
> std::copy_backward(v.begin(), v.begin() + 2, v.end());
> ```

Then it will print `1 2 3 1 2`

What if we want to copy the last 2 elements of the original vector to its beginning?

> **copy the last two to the start**
> ```
> std::copy_backward(v.end() - 2, v.end(), v.begin() + 2);
> ```

Then it will print `4 5 3 4 5`

Now, let us try to be a little more ambitious about using it further. For example, let the *source_start* be 2nd element, *source_end* be 4th element and *destination_end* be 3rd element:

> **destination_end is between source_start and source_end**
> ```
> std::copy_backward(v.begin() + 2, v.begin() + 4, v.begin() + 3);
> ```

When we printed the contents of our vector after this, with gcc 4.8 and clang 3.3, it was:
`1 3 4 4 5`.

But, hold on, we expected it to be:
`1 4 4 4 5`.

Simply, because we were taught that the order of assignment will follow the suite as follows::

std::copy_backward(first, last, result)

$\Longrightarrow$

$$v[resultindex\text{-}1] = v[lastindex\text{-}1];$$
$$v[resultindex\text{-}2] = v[lastindex\text{-}2];$$
$$\dots v[resultindex\text{-}(lastindex\text{-}firstindex)] = v[firstindex];$$

```
std::copy_backward(v.begin() + 2, v.begin() + 4, v.begin() + 3);
```

Here:

$$firstindex = 2, \text{ which is same as v.begin() } + 2$$
$$lastindex = 4, \text{ which is same as v.begin() } + 4$$
$$resultindex = 3, \text{ which is same as v.begin() } +3$$

Hence, we expected the set of assignments to be as follows:

v[resultindex-1] = v[lastindex-1], i.e. v[2] = v[3], i.e. now the original vector : 1 2 3 4 5: would get modified to become 1 2 4 4 5

v[resultindex-2] = v[lastindex-2]; i.e. v[resultindex-(lastindex-firstindex)] = v[firstindex]; i.e. v[1] = v[2], i.e. now the vector should be 1 4 4 4 5

Something was fishy in our understanding or in gcc/clang or everywhere.

1.9 Implementation

So far, we were taught that it may look something like :

Naive guess at the implementation

```
{
    while (source_start != source_end)
    {
        *--destination_end = *--source_end;
    }
    return destination_end;
}
```

1.10 Pictorial Representation

We didn't want to stop here, hence we went ahead with drawing the mental picture of *std::copy_backward* in action:

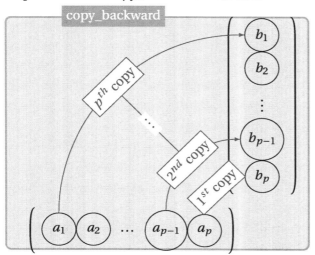

1.11 Another Precondition

Again, we learned a new lesson hard way:

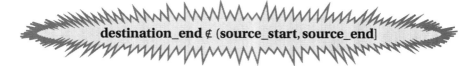

destination_end $\notin$ (source_start, source_end]

As far as the above condition is honored, our understanding was not that challenged.

1.12 More surprises

One thing was very much clear that, the naive looking interface was mere a rosy picture, hiding many unpleasant surprises in its bosom. We thought of delving into these unfathomed depths to the fullest.

How could we achieve this?

We were not very sure, but, all we knew was, we needed to know it at any cost. So the search for a sound interface was about to get started. And, the quest for understanding the relevant supporting language and library features of C++11 was very much at its brim.

So, first of all, we need to take a step to get acquainted with C++11 environment in our neighborhood.

1.13 Source Code Listing

Destination list has no space

```cpp
1  #include <vector>
2  #include <list>
3  #include <algorithm>
4  #include <iostream>
5
6  int main()
7  {
8     std::vector<int> v {1, 2, 3, 4, 5};
9     std::list<int> l;
10    std::copy_backward(v.begin(), v.end(), l.end());
11    for(auto e : l)
12    std::cout << e << " ";
13    std::cout << l.size() << std::endl;
14 }
```

ch1/copy_backward_1_v2.cpp

Listing 1.13.1:   Using copy_backward with no space in destination

Destination list has enough space

```cpp
1  #include <vector>
2  #include <list>
3  #include <algorithm>
4  #include <iostream>
5  #include <cassert>
6
7  int main()
8  {
9      std::vector<int> v = {1, 2, 3, 4, 5};
10     std::list<int> l(v.size()); // enough space
11     std::copy_backward(v.begin(), v.end(), l.end());
12     for(auto e : l)
13         std::cout << e << " ";
14     assert(std::equal(v.begin(), v.end(), l.begin()));
15 }
```

ch1/copy_backward_1.cpp

Listing 1.13.2:   Using copy_backward with enough space in destination

Copying front elements to the back

```
1  #include <vector>
2  #include <list>
3  #include <algorithm>
4  #include <iostream>
5  #include <cassert>
6
7  int main()
8  {
9      std::vector<int> v = {1, 2, 3, 4, 5};
10     std::copy_backward(v.begin(), v.begin() + 2, v.end());
11     for(auto e : v)
12     std::cout << e << " ";
13     assert(std::equal(v.begin(), v.end(), v.begin()));
14 }
```

ch1/copy_backward_2.cpp

Listing 1.13.3:   Usage of copy_backward to copy first 2 elements to back

```
     Copying back elements to the front
 1  #include <vector>
 2  #include <list>
 3  #include <algorithm>
 4  #include <iostream>
 5  #include <cassert>
 6
 7  int main()
 8  {
 9      std::vector<int> v = {1, 2, 3, 4, 5};
10      std::copy_backward(v.end() - 2, v.end(), v.begin() + 2);
11      for(auto e : v)
12          std::cout << e << " ";
13      assert(std::equal(v.begin(), v.end(), v.begin()));
14  }
                        ch1/copy_backward_3.cpp
```

Listing 1.13.4:   Usage of copy_backward to copy last 2 elements to the front

Overlapping source and destination

```cpp
1  #include <vector>
2  #include <list>
3  #include <algorithm>
4  #include <iostream>
5
6  int main()
7  {
8      std::vector<int> v = {1, 2, 3, 4, 5};
9      std::copy_backward(v.begin() + 2, v.begin() + 4, v.begin() + 3);
10     for(auto e : v)
11     std::cout << e << " ";
12 }
```

ch1/copy_backward_4.cpp

Listing 1.13.5:   Usage of copy_backward with overlapping source and destination

Chapter 2

C++11 Environment

2.1   C++11 Compilers

After doing some research, we zeroed on 2 compilers for C++11 experiments on linux distribution Ubuntu 12.04, namely

➡ `http://gcc.gnu.org`

Support of *C++11* in gcc
`http://gcc.gnu.org/projects/cxx0x.html`

19

➡ `http://clang.llvm.org`

Support of *C + +11* in clang
`http://clang.llvm.org/cxx_status.html`

Here is a a nice summary(though a little dated one) of C++11 support by compilers :

`https://wiki.apache.org/stdcxx/C%2B%2B0xCompilerSupport`

2.2 gcc

 is **G**NU **C**ompiler **C**ollection.

2.2.1 Prerequisites

Getting, building and installing the latest of the dependent libraries is mentioned in detail at :
`http://gcc.gnu.org/install/prerequisites.html`, which is summarized below for quick reference.

GMP

GMP is **G**NU **M**ultiple **P**recision Arithmetic Library. Latest source can be download from `http://gmplib.org/`.
Please follow the instructions below to download, configure, build and install it

```
$wget ftp://ftp.gmplib.org/pub/gmp-5.0.5/gmp-5.0.5.tar.bz2
$tar xjvf gmp-5.0.5.tar.bz2
$cd gmp-5.0.5
$./configure
$make -j6
$sudo make install
```

MPFR

MPFR is GNU **M**ultiple **P**recision **F**loating-point computations with correct **R**ounding. Latest source can be download from `http://www.mpfr.org/`.

Please follow the instructions below to download, configure, build and install it

```
$wget http://www.mpfr.org/mpfr-current/mpfr-3.1.1.tar.bz2
$tar xjvf mpfr-3.1.1.tar.bz2
$cd mpfr-3.1.1
$ ./configure --with-gmp-include=/usr/local/include
            --with-gmp-lib=/usr/local/lib
$make -j6
$sudo make install
```

MPC

MPC is GNU **M**ultiple **P**recision **L**ibrary. Latest source can be download from `http://www.multiprecision.org/`.

Please follow the instructions below to download, configure, build and install it

```
$wget http://www.multiprecision.org/mpc/download/mpc-1.0.1.tar.gz
$tar zxvf mpc-1.0.1.tar.gz
$cd mpc-1.0.1
$ ./configure --with-mpfr=/usr/local --with-gmp=/usr/local
$make -j6
$sudo make install
$cd ..
```

2.2.2 Building gcc

Getting the source of gcc from its svn repository is mentioned in the link `http://gcc.gnu.org/svn.html`.

Please follow the instructions below to download, configure, build and install it

```
$pwd
/home/chandu/softwares/
$svn checkout svn://gcc.gnu.org/svn/gcc/trunk gcc-trunk
$mkdir gcc-build
$cd gcc-build
$../gcc-trunk/configure --enable-build-with-cxx
                              --enable-languages=c,c++
$make -j6
$sudo make install
```

gcc version

```
$ gcc --version
gcc (GCC) 4.8.0 20121209 (experimental)
Copyright (C) 2012 Free Software Foundation, Inc.
This is free software; see the source for copying conditions.
There is NO warranty; not even for MERCHANTABILITY or
FITNESS FOR A PARTICULAR PURPOSE.
```

```
$ gcc -v
Using built-in specs.
COLLECT_GCC=gcc
COLLECT_LTO_WRAPPER=
/usr/local/libexec/gcc/x86_64-unknown-linux-gnu/4.8.0/lto-wrapper
Target: x86_64-unknown-linux-gnu
Configured with: ../gcc-trunk/configure --enable-build-with-cxx
--enable-languages=c,c++ : (reconfigured)
../gcc-trunk/configure --enable-build-with-cxx
--enable-languages=c,c++ : (reconfigured)
../gcc-trunk/configure --enable-build-with-cxx
--enable-languages=c,c++
Thread model: posix
gcc version 4.8.0 20121209 (experimental) (GCC)
```

Living on edge

Once it is set-up as mentioned above; to live on the bleeding edge, we can just issue the command *svn update* in the directory *gcc-trunk* , followed by *make -j6* in the directory *gcc-build* and finally install the newly build one by *sudo make install.*

2.2.3 Custom Install

Please note that the above set-up will install the binaries in the directory */usr/local/bin,* the libraries (including libstdc++) in */usr/local/lib* and the headers in */usr/local/include.*

If this is not intended, the desired directory can be given at the time of configuration with the option $--prefix.$

For more options, please run the bash script *configure* with the option $--$ $help$ to customize the build process further.

2.3   clang

clang

Please follow the instructions below to download, configure, build and install it .

2.3.1   LLVM Clang Tools RT

```
$pwd
/home/chandu/softwares
$svn co http://llvm.org/svn/llvm-project/llvm/trunk llvm
$cd llvm/tools
$svn co http://llvm.org/svn/llvm-project/cfe/trunk clang
$cd ../..
$cd llvm/tools/clang/tools
$svn co http://llvm.org/svn/llvm-project/clang-tools-extra/trunk extra
$cd ../../../..
$cd llvm/projects
$svn co http://llvm.org/svn/llvm-project/compiler-rt/trunk compiler-rt
$cd ../..
```

2.3.2   Build and Install Clang

We decided to build the optimized release version:

```
$mkdir llvm-build
$cd llvm-build
$../llvm/configure --enable-optimized
$make -j6
$sudo make install
```

version clang

Checking the clang version (10th Oct 2012)

```
$ clang --version
clang version 3.3 (trunk 169585)
Target: x86_64-unknown-linux-gnu
Thread model: posix
```

Living on edge

Once it is set-up as mentioned above; to live on the bleeding edge, we can just issue *make update* in the directory *llvm-build* to get the latest update on: llvm, clang, runtime: followed by *make -j6* to build it and finally *sudo make install* to install it.

2.4   C++11 Standard Libraries

There are 2 libraries available for C++11:

2.4.1   libstdc++

This is part of the gcc and gets built/installed with the same as well.

By default, this is used by gcc and by clang too.

C++11 Library features in gcc
```
http://gcc.gnu.org/onlinedocs/libstdc++/manual/status.html#
status.iso.200x
```

2.4.2 libc++

`http://libcxx.llvm.org/` : also known as libcxx, which is part of llvm. This is labeled as an optimized implementation of C++11 Standard Library.

Status of C++11 with libc++ can be seen at

- ☞ `http://libcxx.llvm.org/results.Linux.html`

- ☞ `http://libcxx.llvm.org/libcxx_by_chapter.pdf`

2.4.3 Building Installing libc++

Please note that the installation notes available at the site is not for linux-like systems. So kindly please follow the instructions below for building and installing the same on Ubuntu 12.04:

- ☞ Checkout libc++:

  `$svn co http://llvm.org/svn/llvm-project/libcxx/trunk libcxx`

- ☞ Build and install libc++:

```
$pwd
/home/chandu/softwares/
$cd libcxx/lib
$./buildit
```

The above will build the library as *libc++.so.1.0* in the present directory. Now we have to be careful in the installation of libc++, so that it does not conflict with libstdc++.

As shown above, our installation of libstdc++, which was part of the gcc install, was in /usr/local/lib and /usr/local/include : both being part of the standard path already. So, we cannot do the same with libc++.

In order to resolve, we decided to install libc++ in the directory *lopt/clang/lib* and *lopt/clang/include*.

We copied the *libc++.so.1.0* in *lopt/clang/lib*, and the headers from the *lhome/chandu/softwares/libcxx/include* to *lopt/clang/include*.

2.4.4 Post-installation libc++

```
$pwd
/opt/clang/lib
$sudo ln -s libc++.so.1.0 libc++.so
$sudo ln -s libc++.so.1.0 libc++.so.1
$sudo ldconfig
```

2.4.5 Usage of libc++

```
$clang++ -std=c++11 -stdlib=libc++ -I /opt/clang/include/ file.cpp
```

2.5 Usage Summary

So, by now, we have two compilers : gcc 4.8 and clang 3.3 and two implementations of C++11 standard libraries, namely, libstdc++ and libc++.

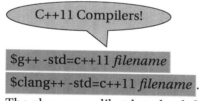

```
$g++ -std=c++11 filename
$clang++ -std=c++11 filename .
```

The above uses libstdc++ by default.

```
$clang++ -std=c++11 -stdlib=libc++ -I /opt/clang/include/ filename
```

Chapter 3

Sound Interface

Using C++11 Features

33 Chapter 4
        Template Aliases

3.1 Concept Design of STL

In our pursuit for a sound interface for std::copy_backward, we stumbled upon the one mentioned in the famous paper:

A Concept Design of STL by *Dr. Bjarne Stroustrup et. al.* at `www.open-std.org/jtc1/sc22/wg21/docs/papers/2012/n3351.pdf`.

After going through the related papers, especially *Design of Concept Li-*

braries for C++ at `http://www.stroustrup.com/sle2011-concepts.` `pdf`, we thought of studying it further with a hands-on approach.

The interface is as follows:

```
1 template<BidirectionalIterator I, BidirectionalIterator Out>
2 requires IndirectlyCopyable<I, Out>
3 Out copy_backward(I first, I last, Out result);
```
Concept Design of STL

3.2 Concept Emulation

In order to understand the ramification of this interface as well as to simulate the stated constraints, well within the confined premises of laid-out C++11, we experimented with quite a lot of libraries, especially the following:

- ➤ Boost Concept Check
  `http://www.boost.org/doc/libs/1_51_0/libs/concept_check/`

- ➤ Concept Traits Library
  `http://neoscientists.org/~tschwinger/boostdev/concept_` `traits/libs/concept_traits/doc/#BoostMPLConceptTraits`

- ➤ `http://catsfoot.sourceforge.net/`

- ➤ Contract++ at `http://contractpp.sourceforge.net/`

- ➤ A template metaprogramming library for concept-based static duck typing in C++11 known as *duck* at `https://github.com/ldionne/` `duck`

- ➤ OpenAxiom at `http://www.open-axiom.org/`

- ➤ Concept-Based Optimizations at
  `https://parasol.tamu.edu/groups/pttlgroup/` `concept-based-optimization/index.html`

➤ Liz parser as mentioned in the paper `https://parasol.tamu.edu/people/villoria/parser-report.pdf` at `http://liz.axiomatics.org/trac/browser`

➤ Elements of Programming parser by Sean Parent at `http://www.elementsofprogramming.com/parser/eop_parser.zip`

➤ Elements of Programming code at `http://www.elementsofprogramming.com/code.html`

➤ Boost TTI Library : Type Traits Introspection : `http://svn.boost.org/svn/boost/trunk/libs/tti/doc/TypeTraitsIntrospection.pdf` at `http://svn.boost.org/svn/boost/trunk/boost/tti/`

➤ Origin C++ Libraries by Andrew Sutton at `http://code.google.com/p/origin/` and at `http://calder.sdml.cs.kent.edu/svn/origin/`

3.3 Origin C++ Libraries

Out of the above, we zeroed-on to nice looking implementation(in progress) approach of *Origin C++ libraries* with a new hope to undertake this journey to a new world. Other reasons for this selection were: no dependency on other libraries as well as heavy and strict usage of C++11 language and library features.

3.3.1 requires

Fortunately, C++11 has one library facility in the name of *std::enable_if* in the header *type_traits*. This could be used to simulate the need of *requires* with the help of another new language feature *Template Aliases*. So we can have the following handy in utilizing these 2 facilities :

```
                        simulation of require
#include <type_traits>

template <bool Condition, typename T = void>
using requires = typename std::enable_if<Condition, T>::type;
                        SFINAE
```

Other thing to keep in mind was to use *requires* to express the following on Input and Output Iterator:

IndirectlyCopyable

Let us march towards the newly introduced language feature : *Template Alias* in the next chapter before we start building *IndirectlyCopyable*.

Part II

Using C++11 Features

Chapter 4

Template Aliases

During early days, this feature was motivated due to the pressing need to allow programmers to create a synonym for a template : class/-function : where some, but not all, actual template arguments are fixed. However, before we jump to understand what *template alias* is and how does it help us better, we need to understand what is *type aliases*, which is part of the *alias declaration*.

4.1 Alias Declaration

In its simple form, *alias declaration* looks like below

> *alias-declaration:*
> > using *identifier attribute-specifier-seq$_{opt}$* = *type-id* ;

So what we conclude from the above is that, an *alias-declaration* is another way to introduce a *typedef-name*. Also it has the same semantics as if it were introduced by the *typedef* specifier.

4.2 Type Alias

Type alias does not define a new type. Hence it does not appear in the *type-id*. An exception-specification cannot appear in an *alias-declaration* as is true in the case of a typedef declaration.

type aliases

```
using vec_int = std::vector<int>;
using func_ptr = void (*)();
using coordinate = std::pair<int, int>;
using Integer = int;
```

simulating template typedef

4.3 Template Alias

In the light of the above, **Template Alias** is a name for a family of type(s). The name of the alias template is a template-name. As an alias-declaration cannot declare a template-id, it is not possible to partially or explicitly specialize an alias template. A template-declaration in which the declaration is an alias-declaration (as shown above) declares the identifier to be an alias template. The point of declaration of a template alias immediately follows the identifier for the alias being declared.

Simple Example

```
template <typename T>
using Vec = std::vector<T>;
```

Now, *Vec* can be used in the same way as *std::vector*, for example, *Vec<int>* is same as *std::vector<int>*.

verify

```
static_assert(std::is_same< Vec<int>, std::vector<int>>::value,
    "Vec<int> should be same as std::vector<int>");
```

Another Example

```
template <template <typename> class TT> struct X { };
template<typename> struct Y { };
template<typename T> using Z = Y<T>;
```

declares y and z to be of the same type

```
X<Y> y;
X<Z> z;
```

verify

```
static_assert(std::is_same< Y<int>, Z<int> >::value,
    "Y<int> is same as Z<int>");
```

more fun

```
template <typename T>
using Dict1 = std::map<std::string, T>;
```

using

```
Dict1<int> int_map;
int_map["First"] = 1;
int_map["Second"] = 2;
```

fun continued

```
template <typename T>
using Dict2 = std::map<T, std::string>;
```

using

```
Dict2<int> int_string_map;
int_string_map[1] = "One";
```

Vec < int > is same as myvec < int, myalloc < int >>

```
1  #include <type_traits>
2
3  template <typename element, typename allocator>
4  struct myvec {};
5
6  template<typename T> struct myalloc {};
7
8  template<typename T>
9  using Vec = myvec<T, myalloc<T>>;
10
11  int main()
12  {
13      // same as myvec<int, myalloc<int>> v1;
14      Vec<int> v1;
15      static_assert(std::is_same <
16                      Vec<int>,
17                      myvec<int, myalloc<int>>
18                  >::value, "");
19  }
```

4.4 Rebind Template

During the initial movement of this concept, the nuances associated with the rebind-style templates were in vogue. So, before *Alias Templates*, the following trickery was in place :

hackery style rebind template

```
template <typename T>
struct allocator
{
    template<typename U>
    struct rebind
    {
        typedef allocator<U> other;
    };
};
```

sample usage

```
allocator<int>::rebind<char>::other x;
```

Thank God, now the same could be cleaned up using template alias like :

cleaner rebind template

```
template <typename T>
struct allocator
{
    template<typename U>
    using rebind = allocator<U>;
};
```

sample usage

```
allocator<int>::rebind<char> x;
```

4.5 Non Deducible Context

Now, let us try to revisit one of our older problems associated with the following snippet:

without template alias

```
template<typename T> struct myalloc {};

template <typename element, typename allocator>
struct myvec {};

template <typename element>
struct Vec
{
    typedef myvec<element, myalloc<element>> type;
};
```

sample usage

```
Vec<int>::type v1;
```

sample function

```
template <typename element>
void f(typename Vec<element>::type& v);
```

usage of the function

```
Vec<int>::type v1;
f(v1);
```

When we tried to compile above code with g++ 4.8,we got the following error:

With clang++ 3.3 we faced following error:

```
without_alias_template_vec.cpp:17:5: error: no matching function
for call to 'f'
    f(v1);
    ^
without_alias_template_vec.cpp:12:34: note: candidate template
ignored: couldn't infer template argument 'element'
template <typename element> void f(typename Vec<element>::type& v);
                                 ^
```

The problem with this kind of usage pattern is two-fold:

- ☞ It causes the template parameters to appear in non-deducible context, i.e., it will not be possible to call the function without explicitly specifying template arguments. In fact this was one of the primary motivations for proposing *template aliases*

- ☞ The syntax is peculiar and inconvenient. We would like to get rid of the nested *::type* call altogether.

As is evident by the understanding of the language feature *Template Alias*, we can overcome the above 2 issues with much ease as seen below:

with template alias

```
template<typename T> struct myalloc {};

template <typename element, typename allocator>
struct myvec {};

template <typename element>
using Vec = myvec<element, myalloc<element>>;

template <typename element> void f(Vec<element>& v);

int main()
{
    Vec<int> v1;
    f(v1);
}
```

If the template parameters are used in deducible contexts in the type-ids, i.e., type expression, as was evident from the example above.Whenever the template alias is used to form a template-id, the values of the corresponding template parameters can be deduced.

There are some cases in which this is not possible. But, nonetheless, this enables writing generic functions which operate on *Vec<T>* in the deducible context.

Moreover, the syntax is highly intuitive because of the implied improvement. We would like to re-iterate here that one of the primary motivating reasons for the proposal of *Template Aliases* was for enabling this kind of argument deduction in the context of the function like mentioned before, so that this call will execute as intended.

We can summarize the above findings as: if the source template parameters, i.e., T as in *myvec < element, myalloc < element >>* could be used in a deducible context in a corresponding function template signature like:

```
                        T is deducible here
template <typename element> void g(myvec <
                        element,
                        myalloc<element>
                    >& v);
```

Then the alias template *Vec<element>* could be used in its place. So wherever T is deducible in the context of the function g above, then T will be deducible in the context of the function f as well.

```
            That is why T is deducible here too
template <typename element> void f(Vec<element>& v);
```

Or, we can say that *Vec<element>* is simply another name for *myvec < element, myalloc < element >>*.

As a consequence

```
                with template alias
template <typename element> void f(Vec<element>& v);
```

is a redeclaration of

```
template <typename element> void f(myvec <
                    element,
                    myalloc<element>
                    >& v);
```

4.5.1 ODR Honored

In fact, have a fresh look at the definitions of the function template f below:

```
template<typename T> struct myalloc {};

template <typename element, typename allocator>
struct myvec {};

template <typename element>
using Vec = myvec<element, myalloc<element>>;

template <typename element>
void f(Vec<element>& v)
{}

template <typename element>
void f(myvec<element, myalloc<element>>& v)
{}
```

When compiled with gcc 4.8, the error is :

```
with_alias_template_vec2.cpp:14:6: error: redefinition of
'template<class element> void f(myvec<element, myalloc<element> >&)'
 void f(myvec<element, myalloc<element>>& v)
      ^
with_alias_template_vec2.cpp:10:6: error: 'template<class element>
void f(Vec<element>&)' previously declared here
```

```
void f(Vec<element>& v)
      ^
```

and, with clang 3.3, the error is :

```
with_alias_template_vec2.cpp:14:6: error: redefinition of 'f'
void f(myvec<element, myalloc<element>>& v)
     ^
with_alias_template_vec2.cpp:10:6: note: previous definition is here
void f(Vec<element>& v)
     ^
1 error generated.
```

4.6   Deducible Context

By now, it looked like we were able to demystify the inherent power of the so called *Template Alias*.

Now, let us turn our eye to a twister :

Specialization
```
template <template <typename> class TT>
void h(TT<int>);
```

Simple Usage
```
Vec<int> v1;
h(v1);
```

But, we were surprised to face the following error with clang 3.3:

```
with_alias_template_vec1.cpp:19:5: error: no matching function
for call to 'h'
   h(v1);
   ^
```

```
with_alias_template_vec1.cpp:10:6: note: candidate template ignored:
failed template argument deduction
void h(TT<int>);
     ^

1 error generated.
```

And with gcc 4.8 :

```
with_alias_template_vec1.cpp: In function 'int main()':
with_alias_template_vec1.cpp:19:9: error: no matching function
for call to 'h(Vec<int>&)'
    h(v1);
      ^
with_alias_template_vec1.cpp:19:9: note: candidate is:
with_alias_template_vec1.cpp:10:6: note:
template<template<class> class TT> void h(TT<int>)
 void h(TT<int>);
      ^
with_alias_template_vec1.cpp:10:6: note:
template argument deduction/substitution failed:
with_alias_template_vec1.cpp:19:9: error: wrong number of
template arguments (2, should be 1)
    h(v1);
      ^
with_alias_template_vec1.cpp:9:37: error: provided for
'template<class> class TT'
 template <template <typename> class TT>
                     ^
```

Hence, *Vec* was not deduced by the call to *h(v1)*, because **An alias template name is never deduced**, i.e., they are as deducible as the equivalent code without using template aliases.

As we know that the specialization of an alias template is not possible. Hence whenever a template-id refers to the specialization-looking usage of an alias template, it is equivalent to the associated type obtained by substitution of its template-arguments for the template-parameters in the type-id of the alias template.

Hence, we need to write the code below to deduce it in this context only:

```
template <template <typename, typename> class TT>
void h1(TT<int, myalloc<int>>);
```

Simple Usage

```
h1(v1);
```

Let us work through a simpler example to understand it better.

deducible context is same as earlier

```
template<typename T>
using ref = T&;

template<typename T>
void f(ref<T> r);

int main()
{
    int x;
    f(x);
}
```

Here, we called f(x) and *T* was deduced perfectly fine. At the point of defi-nition of f only, *ref<T>* was replaced or substituted by the type *T&*. And *T&* is indeed a deducible context.

So, the problem or the area of a deducible context has nothing to do with *Template Aliases*, i.e., neither it is introduced nor aggravated by template alias.

For example :

no template alias here

```
template <typename T>
struct algocoders
{
    typedef T type;
};

template <>
struct algocoders<char>
{
    typedef int type;
};

template <typename T>
using AType = typename algocoders<T>::type;

template <typename T> void f(AType<T>);
```

Now, let us try to use the following :

non-deducible-context

```
int n;
f(n);
```

Here, how could we decide whether we want *T = int* or *T = char*? The whole problem, which is unaffected by template aliases, is that we cannot deduce backwards to all the things that could possibly define something. And the following attempt to declare an template alias is ill-formed :

Ill Formed Template Alias

```
#include <map>

template<class T>
using List = std::pair<T, List<T>*>;
```

Simply because template alias cannot give birth to a type and here *std::pair<T, List<T>*>* is not an existing type since there is no declaration for List available beforehand.

clang 3.3 gives the error:

```
ill_formed_template_alias.cpp:4:27: error: use of undeclared identifier 'List'
using List = std::pair<T, List<T>*>;
                ^
ill_formed_template_alias.cpp:4:32: error: 'T' does not refer to a value
using List = std::pair<T, List<T>*>;
                           ^
ill_formed_template_alias.cpp:3:16: note: declared here
template<class T>
            ^
ill_formed_template_alias.cpp:4:35: error: expected ';' after alias declaration
using List = std::pair<T, List<T>*>;
                              ^
                              ;

3 errors generated.
```

gcc 4.8 error is:

```
ill_formed_template_alias.cpp:4:27: error: 'List' was not declared in this scope
 using List = std::pair<T, List<T>*>;
                 ^
ill_formed_template_alias.cpp:4:33: error: template argument 2 is invalid
 using List = std::pair<T, List<T>*>;
                            ^
ill_formed_template_alias.cpp:4:34: error: expected ';' before '*' token
 using List = std::pair<T, List<T>*>;
                             ^
ill_formed_template_alias.cpp:4:35: error: expected unqualified-id before '>' token
 using List = std::pair<T, List<T>*>;
                             ^
ill_formed_template_alias.cpp:4:35: error: expected constructor, destructor,
 or type conversion before '>' token
```

And, we have to recall that, it is not a new meaning being implied. In fact, it is the same case as that of an attempt below to declare a type alias as well, and this is ill-formed as well:

Ill Formed Type Alias

```
using ListInt = std::pair<int, ListInt<int>>;
```

clang 3.3 error is:

```
ill_formed_template_alias.cpp:6:32: error: use of undeclared identifier
    'ListInt'
using ListInt = std::pair<int, ListInt<int>>;
                                ^
ill_formed_template_alias.cpp:6:43: error: expected '(' for function-style cast
    or type construction
using ListInt = std::pair<int, ListInt<int>>;
                                       ~~~^
```

gcc 4.8 error is:

```
ill_formed_template_alias.cpp:6:32: error: 'ListInt' was not declared in this scope
 using ListInt = std::pair<int, ListInt<int>>;
                                ^
ill_formed_template_alias.cpp:6:43: error: template argument 2 is invalid
 using ListInt = std::pair<int, ListInt<int>>;
                                       ^
```

And, hence is the case with namespace alias as well:

Ill Formed Namespace Alias

```
namespace acode = algocoders;
```

Because there is no existing namespace that the name *algocoders* (on the right hand side) resolves to.

We hope that the concept of aliases is crystal clear by now.
An alias-declaration is a declaration, and not a definition. An alias- declaration introduces a name into a declarative region as an alias for the type designated by the right-hand-side of the declaration.

4.7 Specialization of Template Alias

As we had already mentioned before that *deducibility* and *specializability* can not hold together with *template aliases*, because, template alias doesn't introduce a new template-id, leading to no scope of thought for full or partial specializations in this context.

Since an alias-declaration cannot declare a template-id, **it is not possible to partially or explicitly specialize a template alias**. Though it seems that, to maintain or rather comply with deducibility, specialization of the template alias has been barred, it is still possible to conceive of specialization as a by-product of already existing language constructs, like *traits*, to redirect the template alias to specific specializations.

If we want to specialize a given template alias, then all we have to do is to specialize the source template instead.

For the sake of discussion, let us re-introduce the template alias *Vec* here again:

```
                    Vec as template alias
template<typename T> struct myalloc {};

template <typename element, typename allocator>
struct myvec {};

template <typename element>
using Vec = myvec<element, myalloc<element>>;
```

Let us attempt to specialize our template alias *Vec* as follows:

```
        ill-attempt to specialize template alias for bool
struct vec_bool {};

template <>
using Vec<bool> = vec_bool;
```

With gcc 4.8, the error is

```
specialize_template_alias_vec1.cpp:12:1: error: expected unqualified-id
```

```
before 'using'
 using Vec<bool> = vec_bool;
 ^
```

With clang 3.3, error description was more meaningful :

```
specialize_template_alias_vec1.cpp:11:1: error: explicit specialization of alias
      templates is not permitted
template <>
^~~~~~~~~~~
1 error generated.
```

Instead, let us specialize the very source template for bool as

```
template <>
struct myvec<bool, myalloc<bool>> {};
```

Now we can use *Vec<bool>* with this specialization. In fact, we can have a simplified type-alias as well :

```
using vec_bool = myvec<bool, myalloc<bool>>;
```

Similarly, we can specialize *Vec* for pointer types as well. So, rather than trying to specialize the template alias to *Vec<element*>*, we have to specialize the source template to *myvec<element*, allocator*,i.e.:

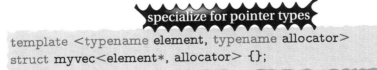

```
template <typename element, typename allocator>
struct myvec<element*, allocator> {};
```

The, *Vec* will pick up this specialized behaviour from *myvec*, and deducibility is retained. Voila !

4.8   Storage Policy

Did we bring ourselves at home, or was it a temporary solace ? We do not know yet, but all we know that it made us very comfortable with the beast-looking concept(at least earlier) known as *Template Alias*.

Suppose, we have a storage policy like :

Storage Policy

```
template <typename StorageType>
struct StoragePolicy
{
    enum { value = sizeof(StorageType) };
};
```

And our favorite template alias as:

convenient template alias

```
template <typename StorageType>
using SP = StoragePolicy<StorageType>;
```

And, we are trying build our logic based on value of the enum as in *value*. Then, our simple usage will be :

simple usage

```
    std::cout << "SP<char>::value = "
            << SP<char>::value << std::endl;
    std::cout << "SP<int>::value = "
            << SP<int>::value << std::endl;
```

```
SP<char>::value = 1
SP<int>::value = 4
```

Let us introduce 2 types to be used for marking left and right in some way:

sentinel types

```
struct Left {};
struct Right {};
```

But, these are not distinguishable from each other, as well as from char:

sentinel types

```
std::cout << "SP<Left>::value = "
         << SP<Left>::value << std::endl;
std::cout << "SP<Right>::value = "
         << SP<Right>::value << std::endl;
```

```
SP<Left>::value = 1
SP<Right>::value = 1
```

Again, it was very tempting to think of specializing *SP* for *Left* and *Right*. But we have learnt by now, that all we have to do is to specialize the source template *StoragePolicy* for these sentinel marker types as:

sentinel types

```
template <>
struct StoragePolicy<Left>
{
    enum { value = -100 };
};

template <>
struct StoragePolicy<Right>
{
    enum { value = 100 };
};
```

Then, our template alias *SP* was very well-behaved as in:

```
                    sentinel types
std::cout << "SP<Left>::value = "
          << SP<Left>::value << std::endl;
std::cout << "SP<Right>::value = "
          << SP<Right>::value << std::endl;
```

```
SP<Left>::value = -100
SP<Right>::value = 100
```

Great so far!!

4.9   Replacing Traits

Let us turn our attention to the missing details in the FAQ at
http://www.stroustrup.com/C++11FAQ.html#template-alias, the
so called infamous *int_exact* example, which tries to name a sized-integer
type, the size of which is expressed as a template argument. This is indeed
a very useful scenario in generic programing context.
All we wanted to achieve was the set of following constructs :

```
            template typedefs : not legal in C++11
template <int> typedef int int_exact;
template <> typedef char int_exact<8>;
template <> typedef short int_exact<16>;
```

But, alas, a typedef cannot be a template because template typedefs is
simply not supported.

4.9.1   Intermediate Traits Idiom

But, still there is hope, courtesy, *Template Aliases*. Though, we cannot
have specializations of template aliases, but, we can have template aliases
to a set of specializations of source templates.

That said, we can design a source template in a form of an intermediate/auxiliary traits template, then specialize it further to represent the specific size-constants.

Primary template Intermediate Traits Idiom

```
template <int>
struct int_exact_traits
{
    typedef int type;
};
```

Specializations of Intermediate Traits Idiom

```
template< >
struct int_exact_traits<8>
{
    typedef char type;
};

template< >
struct int_exact_traits<16>
{
    typedef short type;
};
```

Create a template alias

```
template <int n>
using int_exact = typename int_exact_traits<n>::type;
```

Now, we can use this alias like:

using the template alias

```
    int_exact<8> i8;
```

Wow!!

Let us turn our attention back to the related non-deducible context like:

non-deducible context

```
template <int n>
void f(int_exact<n> &) ;
```

deducibility is simply not possible here

```
int_exact<8> i8;
f(i8);
```

Let us re-iterate here that, non-deducibility is not introduced here because of template alias, rather it was simply aliased to the non-deducibility of the following :

already a non-deducible context

```
template <int n>
void f(typename int_exact_traits<n>::type&);
```

4.10   Revisiting Non-deducible Context

another non-deducible context

```cpp
template <typename T> struct B {};;

template <typename T>
struct A
{
    typedef B<T> type;
};

template <typename T>
using C = typename A<T>::type;

template <typename T>
void f(C<T>);

int main()
{
    B<int> b;
    f(b);
}
```

With, gcc 4.8, the error is :

```
non-deducible-context-1.cpp: In function 'int main()':
non-deducible-context-1.cpp:18:8: error: no matching function for
call to 'f(B<int>&)'
    f(b);
      ^
non-deducible-context-1.cpp:18:8: note: candidate is:
non-deducible-context-1.cpp:13:6: note: template<class T> void f(C<T>)
 void f(C<T>);
      ^
non-deducible-context-1.cpp:13:6: note:
 template argument deduction/substitution failed:
non-deducible-context-1.cpp:18:8: note:   couldn't deduce template parameter 'T'
    f(b);
```

```
      ^
```

With clang 3.3, the error is:

```
non-deducible-context-1.cpp:18:5: error: no matching function for call to 'f'
   f(b);
   ^

non-deducible-context-1.cpp:13:6: note: candidate template ignored: couldn't
      infer template argument 'T'
void f(C<T>);
     ^

1 error generated.
```

To understand it closely, let us look at the following example:

```
primary template
template <typename T>
struct A
{
   typedef T type;
};
```

2 specializations

```
struct B{};
struct C{};

template <>
struct A<B>
{
    typedef int type;
};

template <>
struct A<C>
{
    typedef int type;
};
```

non-deducible context

```
template <typename T>
void f(typename A<T>::type);
```

Now, we have the following situation:

- ✌ A<B>::type is int

- ✌ A<C>::type is also int

So, given that *A<T>::type* is *int*, how would the compiler figure out that whether *T* is *B* or *C*? It cannot even know how many such choices it has, neither can it know the choices themselves(assuming it can know the complete set of choices).

That's why the compiler error says that *A<C>::type* is not deducible. The motivation for this is probably that it isn't technically possible to implement: the compiler would have to instantiate all possible A<T> in order to see if one (and only one) matched the type we passed. And there is an infinite number of possible instantiations of A<T>.

So, **the alias template name cannot be deduced**.

4.11 Template Template Parameters

Matching template template parameters:

matching template template parameters
```
template <template <typename> class X>
struct Y {};

template <typename, typename>
struct Z {};

template <typename T>
using A = Z<T, T>;
```

using template alias A as adapted Z
```
Y<A> a;
```

4.11.1 Loki Smart Pointer

Without *Template Alias,* the usage of loki smart pointers will look like :

without template alias

```
1  #include <loki/SmartPtr.h>
2
3  template <typename T>
4  struct SharedPtr
5  {
6      typedef Loki::SmartPtr <T, Loki::RefCounted> type;
7  };
8
9  template <typename T>
10 struct SharedPtrArray
11 {
12     typedef Loki::SmartPtr <
13                     T,
14                     Loki::RefCounted,
15                     Loki::DisallowConversion,
16                     Loki::AssertCheck,
17                     Loki::ArrayStorage
18                 > type;
19 };
20
21 int main()
22 {
23     SharedPtr<int>::type p;
24     SharedPtrArray<int>::type parr;
25 }
```

```
      with template alias
 1  #include <loki/SmartPtr.h>
 2
 3  template <typename T>
 4      using SharedPtr = Loki::SmartPtr <T, Loki::RefCounted>;
 5
 6  template <typename T>
 7      using SharedPtrArray =
 8          Loki::SmartPtr <
 9                  T,
10                  Loki::RefCounted,
11                  Loki::DisallowConversion,
12                  Loki::AssertCheck,
13                  Loki::ArrayStorage
14              >;
15
16  int main()
17  {
18      SharedPtr<int> p;
19      SharedPtrArray<int> parr;
20  }
```

So, we learned that even a feeble attempt towards getting close to understanding a given language and/or library feature soon starts giving useful
and startling revelations. We witnessed many such unfolding during this
journey and thought of sharing one of these based on explicit template
instantiation in next chapter.

4.12   Source Code Listing

simulating template typedef

```cpp
1  #include <vector>
2  #include <iostream>
3
4  int main()
5  {
6      using vec_int = std::vector<int>;
7      using func_ptr = void (*)();
8      using coordinate = std::pair<int, int>;
9      using Integer = int;
10
11     Integer i = 5;
12 }
```

ch4/alias_type.cpp

Listing 4.12.1:   Using Type Alias and Alias Declaration

```cpp
   Template Alias : Template Template Parameters
 1 #include <type_traits>
 2 #include <vector>
 3
 4 template <typename T>
 5 using Vec = std::vector<T>;
 6
 7 template <template <typename> class TT> struct X { };
 8 template<typename> struct Y { };
 9 template<typename T> using Z = Y<T>;
10
11 int main()
12 {
13    X<Y> y;
14    X<Z> z;
15
16    static_assert(std::is_same< Vec<int>, std::vector<int>>::value,
17       "Vec<int> should be same as std::vector<int>");
18    static_assert(std::is_same< Y<int>, Z<int> >::value,
19       "Y<int> is same as Z<int>");
20 }
                    ch4/alias_template.cpp
```

Listing 4.12.2:   Using Template Alias : Template Template Parameters

```
Template Alias for map
1  #include <type_traits>
2  #include <string>
3  #include <map>
4
5  template <typename T>
6  using Dict1 = std::map<std::string, T>;
7
8  template <typename T>
9  using Dict2 = std::map<T, std::string>;
10
11 int main()
12 {
13    Dict1<int> int_map;
14    int_map["First"] = 1;
15    int_map["Second"] = 2;
16
17    Dict2<int> int_string_map;
18    int_string_map[1] = "One";
19    int_string_map[2] = "Two";
20 }
                    ch4/alias_template_map.cpp
```

Listing 4.12.3:   Map example : template alias

Template Alias for map

```
1  #include <type_traits>
2
3  template <typename element, typename allocator>
4  struct myvec {};
5
6  template<typename T> struct myalloc {};
7
8  template<typename T>
9  using Vec = myvec<T, myalloc<T>>;
10
11 int main()
12 {
13    // same as myvec<int, myalloc<int>> v1;
14    Vec<int> v1;
15    static_assert(std::is_same <
16                  Vec<int>,
17                  myvec<int, myalloc<int>>
18             >::value, "");
19 }
```

ch4/alias_template_vec.cpp

Listing 4.12.4:   Map example : template alias

hackery style rebind template

```cpp
template <typename T>
struct allocator
{
    template<typename U>
    struct rebind
    {
        typedef allocator<U> other;
    };
};

int main()
{
    allocator<int>::rebind<char>::other x;
}
```
ch4/alias_template_rebind1.cpp

Listing 4.12.5:   rebind template : old style

cleaner rebind template

```cpp
template <typename T>
struct allocator
{
    template<typename U>
    using rebind = allocator<U>;
};

int main()
{
    allocator<int>::rebind<char> x;
}
```
ch4/alias_template_rebind2.cpp

Listing 4.12.6:   rebind template with template alias

Using vector without template alias

```cpp
template<typename T> struct myalloc {};

template <typename element, typename allocator>
struct myvec {};

template <typename element>
struct Vec
{
   typedef myvec<element, myalloc<element>> type;
};

template <typename element>
void f(typename Vec<element>::type& v);

int main()
{
   Vec<int>::type v1;
   f(v1);
}
```

ch4/without_alias_template_vec.cpp

Listing 4.12.7:   Using vector without template alias

```
   ┌─────────────────────────────────────┐
   │   Using vector with template alias   │
   └─────────────────────────────────────┘
1  template<typename T> struct myalloc {};
2
3  template <typename element, typename allocator>
4  struct myvec {};
5
6  template <typename element>
7  using Vec = myvec<element, myalloc<element>>;
8
9  template <typename element> void f(Vec<element>& v);
10
11 int main()
12 {
13     Vec<int> v1;
14     f(v1);
15 }
```
ch4/with_alias_template_vec.cpp

Listing 4.12.8:   Using vector with template alias

```
   ┌──────────────────────┐
   │   Deducible Context   │
   └──────────────────────┘
1  template <typename element> void f(Vec<element>& v);
2  template <typename element> void g(myvec <
3                     element,
4                     myalloc<element>
5                     >& v);
6  template <typename element> void f(myvec <
7                     element,
8                     myalloc<element>
9                     >& v);
```
ch4/alias.hpp

Listing 4.12.9:   deducible context

Specialization : Template Alias

```
1  template<typename T> struct myalloc {};
2
3  template <typename element, typename allocator>
4  struct myvec {};
5
6  template <typename element>
7  using Vec = myvec<element, myalloc<element>>;
8
9  template <template <typename> class TT>
10 void h(TT<int>);
11
12 template <template <typename, typename> class TT>
13 void h1(TT<int, myalloc<int>>);
14
15
16 int main()
17 {
18    Vec<int> v1;
19    h(v1);
20    h1(v1);
21 }
```

ch4/with_alias_template_vec1.cpp

Listing 4.12.10:   Specialization : Template Alias

Specialization : Template Alias

```
1  template<typename T> struct myalloc {};
2
3  template <typename element, typename allocator>
4  struct myvec {};
5
6  template <typename element>
7  using Vec = myvec<element, myalloc<element>>;
8
9  template <typename element>
10 void f(Vec<element>& v)
11 {}
12
13 template <typename element>
14 void f(myvec<element, myalloc<element>>& v)
15 {}
```

ch4/with_alias_template_vec2.cpp

Listing 4.12.11:   Specialization : Template Alias

Deducible Context is still intact

```cpp
template<typename T>
using ref = T&;

template<typename T>
void f(ref<T> r);

int main()
{
    int x;
    f(x);
}
```
ch4/alias_template_deducible_1.cpp

Listing 4.12.12:   Deducible Context is honored

Non Deducible Context

```
1  template <typename T>
2  struct algocoders
3  {
4     typedef T type;
5  };
6
7  template <>
8  struct algocoders<char>
9  {
10    typedef int type;
11 };
12
13 template <typename T>
14 using AType = typename algocoders<T>::type;
15
16 template <typename T> void f(AType<T>);
17
18 int main()
19 {
20    int n;
21    f(n);
22 }
```

ch4/alias_template_deducible_2.cpp

Listing 4.12.13:   Non Deducible Context

Ill Formed Namespace Alias

```
1 #include <map>
2
3 template<class T>
4 using List = std::pair<T, List<T>*>;
5
6 using ListInt = std::pair<int, ListInt<int>>;
7
8 namespace acode = algocoders;
```

ch4/ill_formed_template_alias.cpp

Listing 4.12.14:   Ill Formed Namespace Alias

Vec as template alias

```
1 template<typename T> struct myalloc {};
2
3 template <typename element, typename allocator>
4 struct myvec {};
5
6 template <typename element>
7 using Vec = myvec<element, myalloc<element>>;
8
9 struct vec_bool {};
10
11 template <>
12 using Vec<bool> = vec_bool;
```

ch4/specialize_template_alias_vec1.cpp

Listing 4.12.15:   Vec as template alias

Vec as template alias

```cpp
template<typename T> struct myalloc {};

template <typename element, typename allocator>
struct myvec {};

template <typename element>
using Vec = myvec<element, myalloc<element>>;

template <>
struct myvec<bool, myalloc<bool>> {};

using vec_bool = myvec<bool, myalloc<bool>>;

Vec<bool> vbool;
Vec<int> vint;
```

ch4/specialize_template_alias_vec2.cpp

Listing 4.12.16: Vec as template alias

specialization of template alias

```cpp
template<typename T> struct myalloc {};

template <typename element, typename allocator>
struct myvec {};

template <typename element>
using Vec = myvec<element, myalloc<element>>;

template <typename element, typename allocator>
struct myvec<element*, allocator> {};
```

ch4/specialize_template_alias_vec3.cpp

Listing 4.12.17: specialization of template alias

storage policy: template alias

```cpp
1  #include <iostream>
2
3  template <typename StorageType>
4  struct StoragePolicy
5  {
6      enum { value = sizeof(StorageType) };
7  };
8
9  template <typename StorageType>
10 using SP = StoragePolicy<StorageType>;
11
12 struct Left {};
13 struct Right {};
14
15 template <>
16 struct StoragePolicy<Left>
17 {
18     enum { value = -100 };
19 };
20
21 template <>
22 struct StoragePolicy<Right>
23 {
24     enum { value = 100 };
25 };
```

ch4/specialize_template_alias.cpp

storage policy: template alias

```
26
27  int main()
28  {
29      std::cout << "SP<char>::value = "
30              << SP<char>::value << std::endl;
31      std::cout << "SP<int>::value = "
32              << SP<int>::value << std::endl;
33      std::cout << "SP<Left>::value = "
34              << SP<Left>::value << std::endl;
35      std::cout << "SP<Right>::value = "
36              << SP<Right>::value << std::endl;
37  }
```

ch4/specialize_template_alias.cpp

Listing 4.12.18:   storage policy: template alias

template typedefs : not legal in C++11

```
1  template <int> typedef int int_exact;
2  template <> typedef char int_exact<8>;
3  template <> typedef short int_exact<16>;
```

ch4/int_exact_typedefs.hpp

Listing 4.12.19:   template typedefs : not legal in C++11

Intermediate Traits Idiom

```
1  template <int>
2  struct int_exact_traits
3  {
4     typedef int type;
5  };
6
7  template< >
8  struct int_exact_traits<8>
9  {
10     typedef char type;
11  };
12
13  template< >
14  struct int_exact_traits<16>
15  {
16     typedef short type;
17  };
18
19  template <int n>
20  using int_exact = typename int_exact_traits<n>::type;
21
22  template <int n>
23  void f(int_exact<n> &) ;
24
25  int main()
26  {
27     int_exact<8> i8;
28     f(i8);
29  }
```

ch4/specialize_int_exact_traits.cpp

Listing 4.12.20:   Intermediate Traits Idiom

already a non-deducible context

```
1  template <int n>
2  void f(typename int_exact_traits<n>::type&);
```

ch4/non-deducible-context.hpp

Listing 4.12.21:   already a non-deducible context

another non-deducible context

```
1  template <typename T> struct B {};
2
3  template <typename T>
4  struct A
5  {
6      typedef B<T> type;
7  };
8
9  template <typename T>
10 using C = typename A<T>::type;
11
12 template <typename T>
13 void f(C<T>);
14
15 int main()
16 {
17     B<int> b;
18     f(b);
19 }
```

ch4/non-deducible-context-1.hpp

Listing 4.12.22:   another non-deducible context

illustrating non-deducible context

```
1 template <typename T>
2 struct A
3 {
4    typedef T type;
5 };
6
7 struct B{};
8 struct C{};
9
10 template <>
11 struct A<B>
12 {
13    typedef int type;
14 };
15
16 template <>
17 struct A<C>
18 {
19    typedef int type;
20 };
21
22 template <typename T>
23 void f(typename A<T>::type);
24
25 int main()
26 {
27    A<int>::type i;
28    f(i);
29 }
```

ch4/non-deducible-context-2.hpp

Listing 4.12.23:   illustrating non-deducible context

Matching template template parameters

```
1  template <template <typename> class X>
2  struct Y {};
3
4  template <typename, typename>
5  struct Z {};
6
7  template <typename T>
8  using A = Z<T, T>;
9
10 Y<A> a;
```

ch4/template_template_param_alias_templates.cpp

Listing 4.12.24:   using template alias A as adapted Z

Loki Smart Pointer without template alias

```
1  #include <loki/SmartPtr.h>
2
3  template <typename T>
4  struct SharedPtr
5  {
6     typedef Loki::SmartPtr <T, Loki::RefCounted> type;
7  };
8
9  template <typename T>
10 struct SharedPtrArray
11 {
12    typedef Loki::SmartPtr <
13                  T,
14                  Loki::RefCounted,
15                  Loki::DisallowConversion,
16                  Loki::AssertCheck,
17                  Loki::ArrayStorage
18                > type;
19 };
20
21 int main()
22 {
23    SharedPtr<int>::type p;
24    SharedPtrArray<int>::type parr;
25 }
```

ch4/loki_smart_ptr.cpp

Listing 4.12.25:   Loki Smart Pointer without template alias

Loki Smart Pointer with template alias

```
1  #include <loki/SmartPtr.h>
2
3  template <typename T>
4     using SharedPtr = Loki::SmartPtr <T, Loki::RefCounted>;
5
6  template <typename T>
7     using SharedPtrArray =
8        Loki::SmartPtr <
9                T,
10               Loki::RefCounted,
11               Loki::DisallowConversion,
12               Loki::AssertCheck,
13               Loki::ArrayStorage
14          >;
15
16  int main()
17  {
18     SharedPtr<int> p;
19     SharedPtrArray<int> parr;
20  }
```

ch4/loki_smart_ptr_alias.cpp

Listing 4.12.26:   Loki Smart Pointer with template alias

Chapter 5

Private Cast

fter mastering one of the language features of C++11, namely *Template Alias*, which helped us reveal the concept of *Deducibility* vs *Specializability*.

And, strange thing was, this was not something new to C++11 per se. Nonetheless, it was unveiled due to the power enabled by template alias. This lead us to simplified expressions beyond imagination. We were sure that there could be many such things under the hood, which were buried deep within the strange looking *normadic* sentences of the C++11 standard, waiting to be revealed, only if exposed to its direct (though constrained) usage opportunities.

5.1   Explicit Instantiation

So, we were quite watchful this time while perusing through the standard. We came across the following sentence in Section 14.7.2 *Explicit instantiation*, paragraph 12 of the standard :

The usual access checking rules do not apply to names used to specify explicit instantiations.

[Note: In particular, the template arguments and names used in the function declarator (including parameter types, return types and exception specifications) may be **private types or objects which would normally not be accessible** and **the template may be a member template or member function which would not normally be accessible**. — end note]

This was highly astonishing to us. We started wondering if it could mean to help us build a compile-time framework to change the *private* access rules for a given class in the context of names used to specify explicit instantiations.

Let us have a simple class with just one private member data and one private member function. This we will try to use in a context of explicit instantiation outside this class.

Simple Class

```
struct A
{
    A(int i) : private_member_data(i) {}

private:
    int private_member_data;
    void private_member_function() {}
};
```

5.2 Pointer to member

class template with parameter as pointer to member data of A

```
template <int A::*member_data>
struct B{};
```

Sample Usage

```
B<&A::private_member_data> b;
```

error with clang 3.3 is:

```
private_access_1.cpp:18:11: error: 'private_member_data' is a private member of
   'A'
  B<&A::private_member_data> b;
      ^
private_access_1.cpp:6:9: note: declared private here
   int private_member_data;
       ^
```

error with gcc 4.8 is:

```
private_access_1.cpp:6:9: error: 'int A::private_member_data' is private
   int private_member_data;
       ^
private_access_1.cpp:18:5: error: within this context
   B<&A::private_member_data> b;
     ^
```

Same is the case with the below as well:

class template with parameter as pointer to member function of A

```
template <void (A::*member_function)()>
struct C{};
```

```
C<&A::private_member_function> c;
```

So far, the above case is in line with the usual accessibility rules related to private stuff of a given class. So we got rid of the above kind of usage and proceeded towards explicit instantiation like:

Explicit Instantiation with private member data
```
template struct B<&A::private_member_data>;
```

Now, there was no error.

Explicit Instantiation with private member function
```
template struct C<&A::private_member_function>;
```

No error this time as well. So this was in sync with the above stated standard, i.e., the usual access checking rules didn't apply to names used to specify explicit instantiations.

5.3 Access Checking Rules

A quick look inside the relevant changes in the code base of *clang* is at `http://llvm.org/viewvc/llvm-project/cfe/trunk/lib/Parse/ParseDeclCXX.cpp?r1=106496&r2=106993&diff_format=h`

A closer look is:

```
                  llvm/tools/clang/lib/Parse/ParseDeclCXX.cpp
// C++03 [temp.explicit] 14.7.2/8:
//   The usual access checking rules do not apply to names
//   used to specify explicit instantiations.
//
// As an extension we do not perform access checking on the
// names used to specify explicit specializations either.
// This is important to allow specializing traits classes
// for private types.
//
// Note that we don't suppress if this turns out to be
// an elaborated type specifier.

bool shouldDelayDiagsInTag =
  (TemplateInfo.Kind ==
      ParsedTemplateInfo::ExplicitInstantiation ||
   TemplateInfo.Kind ==
      ParsedTemplateInfo::ExplicitSpecialization);

SuppressAccessChecks diagsFromTag(
          *this, shouldDelayDiagsInTag);
```

As could be seen in the changes above, this allows the very common practice of specializing trait classes to work for private, internal types. Thereby opening the ways to see explicit specializations as a special case of explicit instantiations.

Here is a link to the relevant commit-changes: `http://lists.cs.uiuc.edu/pipermail/cfe-commits/Week-of-Mon-20100628/031632.html`

And a direct link to doxygen-based latest code is :
`http://clang.llvm.org/doxygen/ParseDeclCXX_8cpp_source.html`
Let us work with some code snippets to understand it better:

Sample snippet

```
struct X
{
private:
    template <typename T> class Y {};
};

struct A
{
private:
    struct B {};
    struct C {};
};
```

explicit instantiation : access rules is not at force

```
template struct X::Y<A::B>;
```

explicit specialization: access rules is not at force

```
template <> class X::Y<A::C> {};
```

All of these re-iterate the same story. And it echoes itself :

Sample Code

```
struct A
{
private:
    struct Private {};
public:
    typedef Private Public;
};

template <typename T>
struct A_x
{
    static A_x<A::Public> make() { return A_x<A::Public>(); }
};
```

explicit instantiation is ok

```
template struct A_x<A::Private>;
```

This should be an error

```
template struct A_x<A::Private> A_x<int>::make();
```

But, alas! both clang 3.3 and gcc 4.8 accept this usage silently.

Another Sample Code

```
template <typename T>
struct B_x
{
private:
    static B_x<A::Public> make();
};
```

```
                 explicit specialization is fine
template <>
struct B_x<A::Private>
{
    B_x(int x) {}
};
```

```
                 This should be an error
template <>
struct B_x<A::Private> B_x<int>::make()
{
    return B_x<A::Public>(0);
}
```

But, gcc 4.8 accepts this too. Thanks God, clang 3.3 yields the error as expected:

```
private_access_5.cpp:41:15: error: 'Private' is a private member of 'A'
struct B_x<A::Private> B_x<int>::make()
          ^
private_access_5.cpp:4:12: note: declared private here
    struct Private {};
           ^
1 error generated.
```

5.4 Casting Private Member Data

This led us to sniff our wit to a related end to generalize this magic some-what like an attempt to build a compile-time-framework which can be used to garner an insight to have a private cast utility at our disposal. This can be used to mark the private members of a given class. But, wait! We are still far from this fulfillment. Let us draw ourselves closer at a slow and controlled pace.

Let us revisit our sample class A:

Sample Class

```
struct A
{
    A(int i) : private_member_data(i) {}

private:
    int private_member_data;
};
```

All we wished was to access the private data member *private_member_data* by this magic. And we had learnt that pointer to members can cross the barriers imposed by access levels.

5.4.1 Tag Type for Private Data

The very step was to have a pointer to this data member. As it was very obvious to do it outside the class *A*. Therefore we did it like this:

Wrapper Class to hold pointer to A's data member

```
struct A_x
{
    typedef int (A::*type);
};
```

So, *A_x* is a kind of a tag type : *Tag::type*: for *A::private_member_data*. Next, we need is a static data member of type *Tag::type*, which will be used to store the address of a private data member per se:

store house of private members

```
template <typename Tag>
struct B1
{
    static typename Tag::type val;
};
```

define the static part

```
template <typename Tag>
typename Tag::type B1<Tag>::val;
```

Again, we need someone who can initialize this, i.e., *B1<Tag>::value* with address of the private data member. Hence this is the only type which can be used to achieve this effect with the explicit template instantiation.

Initialize the static part with the pointer to private member

```
template <typename Tag, typename Tag::type x>
struct B2
{
    B2() { B1<Tag>::val = x; }
    static B2 instance;
};
```

define the static part

```
template <typename Tag, typename Tag::type x>
B2<Tag, x> B2<Tag, x>::instance;
```

Now, let the real magic start by explicit instantiation, which is a mechanism to help pass the address of a private data member.

define the static part

```
template struct B2<A_x, &A::private_member_data>;
```

This will generate the static *::instance* which in turn initializes the *B1<Tag>::val*.

Now is the time to access the private member of the class *A* using the private member pointer syntax like:

Access the private Member

```
int main()
{
    A a(10);
    std::cout << a.*B1<A_x>::val << std::endl;
}
```

5.5 private_cast framework

In a nutshell, the infrastructure of *private_cast* looks like:

private_cast

```
3  template <typename Tag>
4  struct private_cast
5  {
6      static typename Tag::type val;
7  };
8
9  template <typename Tag>
10 typename Tag::type private_cast<Tag>::val;
11
12
13 template <typename Tag, typename Tag::type x>
14 struct private_cast_helper
15 {
16     private_cast_helper() { private_cast<Tag>::val = x; }
17     static private_cast_helper instance;
18 };
19
20 template <typename Tag, typename Tag::type x>
21 private_cast_helper<Tag, x>
22 private_cast_helper<Tag, x>::instance;
```

5.6   Using private_cast

If we have a class like this :

Sample Class

```cpp
struct A
{
   A(int i) : private_member_data(i) {}

private:
   int private_member_data;
   void private_member_function()
   {
      std::cout << "private_member_data is : "
      << private_member_data << std::endl;
   }
};
```

for which we want to circumvent the private access levels for both the data member and the member function.
Then in that case all we have to do, is to write access tags for each of these like:

access tags

```cpp
struct A_x { typedef int (A::*type); };

struct A_f { typedef void (A::*type)(); };
```

And, invoke the explicit template instantiations as:

explicit template instantiations

```
template struct private_cast_helper <
                A_x, &A::private_member_data
            >;
template struct private_cast_helper <
                A_f, &A::private_member_function
            >;
```

Now, we can easily access private members as follows:

Usage

```
int main()
{
    A a(10);

    std::cout << a.*private_cast<A_x>::val << std::endl;
    a.*private_cast<A_x>::val = 20;
    std::cout << a.*private_cast<A_x>::val << std::endl;
    (a.*private_cast<A_f>::val)();
}
```

5.7 Another private_cast

After this, we became very ambitious and took another plunge along seem-
ingly similar lines :

another private_cast

```
template<typename T, T x> struct private_cast { static T val; };

template<typename T, T x> T private_cast<T, x>::val = x;
```

Attempt to use

```cpp
int main()
{
    A a(10);

    std::cout <<
    (a.*private_cast <
        decltype(&A::private_member_data),
        &A::private_member_data
    >::val)
    << std::endl;

    (a.*private_cast <
        decltype(&A::private_member_function),
        &A::private_member_function
    >::val)();
}
```

To our surprise, gcc 4.8 compiled this code and executed as expected. Alas! clang 3.3 gave the relevant error as follows:

```
private_access_7.cpp:26:22: error: 'private_member_data' is a private
member of 'A'
        decltype(&A::private_member_data),
                     ^
private_access_7.cpp:12:9: note: declared private here
    int private_member_data;
        ^
private_access_7.cpp:27:13: error: 'private_member_data' is a private
member of 'A'
        &A::private_member_data
            ^
private_access_7.cpp:12:9: note: declared private here
    int private_member_data;
        ^
private_access_7.cpp:32:22: error: 'private_member_function' is a
private member of 'A'
        decltype(&A::private_member_function),
```

```
                     ^
private_access_7.cpp:13:10: note: declared private here
    void private_member_function()
        ^
private_access_7.cpp:33:13: error: 'private_member_function' is a
private member of 'A'
        &A::private_member_function
            ^
private_access_7.cpp:13:10: note: declared private here
    void private_member_function()
        ^
4 errors generated.
```

We toned down ourselves with this audacity and confined ourselves to the realm of explicit template instantiations. But static stuff started bothering us with the notorious static initialization fiasco. So we went ahead with another attempt to simulate the *private_cast* discussed in the next section.

5.8 Refined private_cast

refined private_cast
```
template <typename Tag, typename Tag::type x>
struct private_cast
{
    friend typename Tag::type get(Tag) { return x; }
};
```

access tag and explicit template instantiation
```
struct A_x
{
    typedef int (A::*type);
    friend type get(A_x);
};

template struct private_cast<A_x, &A::private_member_data>;
```

Usage

```
int main()
{
    A a(10);

    std::cout << a.*get(A_x()) << std::endl;
    a.*get(A_x())  = 20;
    std::cout << a.*get(A_x()) << std::endl;
}
```

To help us define the access tags in a simpler way, we can have:

refined private_cast_helper

```
template<typename Tag, typename Member>
struct private_cast_helper
{
    typedef Member type;
    friend type get(Tag);
};
```

writing access tags becomes cool

```
struct A_x : private_cast_helper<A_x, int A::*> {};
```

The set of exercises helped us stimulate our intellect to a different degree and kept us on toe for learning in an open-ended way.

We learned that the rules associated with the explicit template instantiations is a powerful beast, hinting that similar will be the fate with explicit template specializations as well.

Also please remember that this is just a tip of the iceberg as far as foundation of algorithms is concerned. Let us turn the leaf to the hot-spot, i.e., our infamous example of **copy_backward** in the forthcoming chapter, restarting with understanding the meaning of *requires*-based constraining.

5.9   Source Code Listing

Attempt to access private

```
1  struct A
2  {
3     A(int i) : private_member_data(i) {}
4
5  private:
6     int private_member_data;
7     void private_member_function() {}
8  };
9
10 template <int A::*member_data>
11 struct B{};
12
13 template <void (A::*member_function)()>
14 struct C{};
15
16 int main()
17 {
18    B<&A::private_member_data> b;
19    C<&A::private_member_function> c;
20 }
```

ch5/private_access_1.cpp

Listing 5.9.1:   Attempt to access private

Explicit Instantiation with private member

```
1  struct A
2  {
3      A(int i) : private_member_data(i) {}
4
5  private:
6      int private_member_data;
7      void private_member_function() {}
8  };
9
10 template <int A::*member_data>
11 struct B{};
12
13 template <void (A::*member_function)()>
14 struct C{};
15
16 template struct B<&A::private_member_data>;
17 template struct C<&A::private_member_function>;
18
19 int main()
20 {
21 }
```

ch5/private_access_2.cpp

Listing 5.9.2:   Explicit Instantiation with private member

llvm/tools/clang/lib/Parse/ParseDeclCXX.cpp

```
1073   // C++03 [temp.explicit] 14.7.2/8:
1074   //   The usual access checking rules do not apply to names
1075   //   used to specify explicit instantiations.
1076   //
1077   // As an extension we do not perform access checking on the
1078   // names used to specify explicit specializations either.
1079   // This is important to allow specializing traits classes
1080   // for private types.
1081   //
1082   // Note that we don't suppress if this turns out to be
1083   // an elaborated type specifier.
1084
1085   bool shouldDelayDiagsInTag =
1086     (TemplateInfo.Kind ==
1087         ParsedTemplateInfo::ExplicitInstantiation ||
1088     TemplateInfo.Kind ==
1089         ParsedTemplateInfo::ExplicitSpecialization);
1090
1091   SuppressAccessChecks diagsFromTag(
1092               *this, shouldDelayDiagsInTag);
1093
1094   ParsedAttributesWithRange attrs(AttrFactory);
1095   // If attributes exist after tag, parse them.
1096   if (Tok.is(tok::kw___attribute))
1097     ParseGNUAttributes(attrs);
1098
1099   // If declspecs exist after tag, parse them.
1100   while (Tok.is(tok::kw___declspec))
1101     ParseMicrosoftDeclSpec(attrs);
```

ch5/ParseDeclCXX.cpp

Listing 5.9.3:   llvm/tools/clang/lib/Parse/ParseDeclCXX.cpp

```
                        access rules is not at force
1  struct X
2  {
3  private:
4      template <typename T> class Y {};
5  };
6
7  struct A
8  {
9  private:
10     struct B {};
11     struct C {};
12 };
13
14 template struct X::Y<A::B>;
15
16 template <> class X::Y<A::C> {};
```
ch5/private_access_4.cpp

Listing 5.9.4:   explicit instantiation and specialization

demo of access rules

```
1  struct A
2  {
3  private:
4      struct Private {};
5  public:
6      typedef Private Public;
7  };
8
9  template <typename T>
10 struct A_x
11 {
12     static A_x<A::Public> make() { return A_x<A::Public>(); }
13 };
14
15 template struct A_x<A::Private>;
16
17 template struct A_x<A::Private> A_x<int>::make();
18
19 struct B
20 {
21 private:
22     struct Private {};
23 public:
24     typedef Private Public;
25 };
26
27 template <typename T>
28 struct B_x
29 {
30 private:
31     static B_x<A::Public> make();
32 };
```

ch5/private_access_5.cpp

```
         demo of access rules
33
34 template <>
35 struct B_x<A::Private>
36 {
37    B_x(int x) {}
38 };
39
40 template <>
41 struct B_x<A::Private> B_x<int>::make()
42 {
43    return B_x<A::Public>(0);
44 }
                  ch5/private_access_5.cpp
```

Listing 5.9.5:   demo of access rules

Accessing Private Members

```cpp
1  #include <iostream>
2
3  struct A
4  {
5      A(int i) : private_member_data(i) {}
6
7  private:
8      int private_member_data;
9  };
10
11 struct A_x
12 {
13     typedef int (A::*type);
14 };
15
16 template <typename Tag>
17 struct B1
18 {
19     static typename Tag::type val;
20 };
21
22 template <typename Tag>
23 typename Tag::type B1<Tag>::val;
24
25
26 template <typename Tag, typename Tag::type x>
27 struct B2
28 {
29     B2() { B1<Tag>::val = x; }
30     static B2 instance;
31 };
32
33 template <typename Tag, typename Tag::type x>
34 B2<Tag, x> B2<Tag, x>::instance;
35
36 template struct B2<A_x, &A::private_member_data>;
```

ch5/private_access_3.cpp

Accessing Private Members

```
37
38
39 int main()
40 {
41    A a(10);
42    std::cout << a.*B1<A_x>::val << std::endl;
43 }
```

ch5/private_access_3.cpp

Listing 5.9.6:   Accessing Private Members

private cast framework

```cpp
#include <iostream>

template <typename Tag>
struct private_cast
{
    static typename Tag::type val;
};

template <typename Tag>
typename Tag::type private_cast<Tag>::val;


template <typename Tag, typename Tag::type x>
struct private_cast_helper
{
    private_cast_helper() { private_cast<Tag>::val = x; }
    static private_cast_helper instance;
};

template <typename Tag, typename Tag::type x>
private_cast_helper<Tag, x>
private_cast_helper<Tag, x>::instance;

struct A
{
    A(int i) : private_member_data(i) {}

private:
    int private_member_data;
    void private_member_function()
    {
        std::cout << "private_member_data is : "
                  << private_member_data << std::endl;
    }
};
```

ch5/private_access_6.cpp

```
     private cast framework

36
37  struct A_x { typedef int (A::*type); };
38
39  struct A_f { typedef void (A::*type)(); };
40
41  template struct private_cast_helper <
42                     A_x, &A::private_member_data
43                  >;
44  template struct private_cast_helper <
45                     A_f, &A::private_member_function
46                  >;
47
48  int main()
49  {
50     A a(10);
51
52     std::cout << a.*private_cast<A_x>::val << std::endl;
53     a.*private_cast<A_x>::val = 20;
54     std::cout << a.*private_cast<A_x>::val << std::endl;
55     (a.*private_cast<A_f>::val)();

                  ch5/private_access_6.cpp
```

Listing 5.9.7:   private cast framework

trying to private cast

```
1  #include <iostream>
2
3  template<typename T, T x> struct private_cast { static T val; };
4
5  template<typename T, T x> T private_cast<T, x>::val = x;
6
7  struct A
8  {
9     A(int i) : private_member_data(i) {}
10
11 private:
12    int private_member_data;
13    void private_member_function()
14    {
15       std::cout << "private_member_data is : "
16               << private_member_data << std::endl;
17    }
18 };
19
20
21 int main()
22 {
23    A a(10);
24
25    std::cout <<
26    (a.*private_cast <
27       decltype(&A::private_member_data),
28       &A::private_member_data
29    >::val)
30    << std::endl;
31
32    (a.*private_cast <
33       decltype(&A::private_member_function),
34       &A::private_member_function
35    >::val)();
36 }
```

ch5/private_access_7.cpp

Listing 5.9.8:   trying to private cast

refined private cast

```cpp
1  #include <iostream>
2
3  template <typename Tag, typename Tag::type x>
4  struct private_cast
5  {
6      friend typename Tag::type get(Tag) { return x; }
7  };
8
9  struct A
10 {
11     A(int i) : private_member_data(i) {}
12
13 private:
14     int private_member_data;
15 };
16
17 struct A_x
18 {
19     typedef int (A::*type);
20     friend type get(A_x);
21 };
22
23 template struct private_cast<A_x, &A::private_member_data>;
24
25 int main()
26 {
27     A a(10);
28
29     std::cout << a.*get(A_x()) << std::endl;
30     a.*get(A_x()) = 20;
31     std::cout << a.*get(A_x()) << std::endl;
32 }
```

ch5/private_access_8.cpp

Listing 5.9.9:   refined private cast

refined private cast helper

```
1  #include <iostream>
2
3  template <typename Tag, typename Tag::type x>
4  struct private_cast
5  {
6      friend typename Tag::type get(Tag) { return x; }
7  };
8
9  template<typename Tag, typename Member>
10 struct private_cast_helper
11 {
12     typedef Member type;
13     friend type get(Tag);
14 };
15
16 struct A
17 {
18     A(int i) : private_member_data(i) {}
19
20 private:
21     int private_member_data;
22 };
23
24 struct A_x : private_cast_helper<A_x, int A::*> {};
25
26 template struct private_cast<A_x, &A::private_member_data>;
27
28 int main()
29 {
30     A a(10);
31
32     std::cout << a.*get(A_x()) << std::endl;
33     a.*get(A_x()) = 20;
34     std::cout << a.*get(A_x()) << std::endl;
35 }
```

ch5/private_access_9.cpp

Listing 5.9.10:   refined private cast helper

Chapter 6

requires clause

Concept Design

131 Chapter 7
         Type Functions

As we learned so far about simulation of the *requires* clause is with the blend of 2 facilities provided with C++11, namely,

☞ library facility *std::enable_if* in the header $< type\_traits >$, which provides handy wrapper for utilizing

SFINAE: **Substitution Failure Is Not An Error** .

☞ language facility *Template Aliases* to help us wrap the above library facility with the expected pseudonym **requires**.

```
#include <type_traits>

template <bool Condition, typename T = void>
using requires = typename std::enable_if<Condition, T>::type;
```

6.1 SFINAE

What is the enabling mechanism here as far as *sfinae* is concerned?

It is very simple.

Please note that it applies to help build a set of inclusion and/or exclusion of the following:

⟶ a function template overloading, or

⟶ a class template specialization

It gets excluded from the (overload in case of function templates) resolution set instead of a compiler error in case of formation of invalid argument or return type(s) during the instantiation phase.

Quick sfinae refresher:

```
                    basic example of sfinae on return type
int f(int i) { return i; }

template <typename T>
typename T::type f(T i) { return i; }

int main()
{
    f(5);
}
```

The above example runs fine because during instantiation phase, the second definition of the function f gets excluded from the overload resolution set due to invalid return type : *int::type*.

A substitution failure results into elimination of an overload or specialization from a candidate set. So, the alias requires refers to T, only in case of B(the condition as a first parameter) being true(of course at compile time).

Let us look at another simple example:

```
naive code without sfinae
#include <iostream>
#include <iomanip>

template <typename T>
bool odd(T n) { return n & 1; }

int main()
{
    std::cout << std::boolalpha;

    std::cout << odd(1) << std::endl;
    std::cout << odd(2) << std::endl;
    std::cout << odd(1.2) << std::endl;
}
```

clang++ give the error as:

```
requires_integer1.cpp:5:26: error: invalid operands to binary expression
    ('double' and 'double')
bool odd(T n) { return n & 1; }
                       ~ ^ ~
requires_integer1.cpp:13:18: note: in instantiation of function template
    specialization 'odd<double>' requested here
    std::cout << odd(1.2) << std::endl;
                 ^
1 error generated.
```

Call to *odd(1.2)* results into calling the definition of the function odd, though we could have wished simply to ignore that definition because that was meant only with integral types, at least intent wise. But the expression for this tacit intent was missing in the above code.

6.2 constexpr wrapper

With the help of *requires*, we can express the intent in 2 steps:
☞ Distinguish integral types from the non-integral types. Luckily, C++11
provides us **std::is_integral<T>** as part of *type_traits* bundle.

Integer trait

```
template <typename T>
constexpr bool Integer() { return std::is_integral<T>::value; }
```

Returns true if T is an integral type, i.e. signed or unsigned, possibly cv-
qualified, bool, char, short, int, long or long long.
☞ Use sfinae-enriched return type to let the function *odd* be only a viable
candidate when the expression *Integer<T>()* evaluates to true

sfinae bound meta-function

```
template <typename T>
requires<Integer<T>(), T> odd(T n) { return n & 1; }
```

clang++ give the error as:

```
requires_integer2.cpp:18:18: error: no matching function for call to 'odd'
    std::cout << odd(1.2) << std::endl;
                 ^ ~~
./require.hpp:4:42: note: candidate template ignored:
 disabled by 'enable_if'
    [with T = double]
using requires = typename std::enable_if<Condition, T>::type;
                                  ^
1 error generated.
```

And this is as expected as it resulted into exclusion of the function odd
from the candidate set altogether. Cool one !

Sadly, g++ (GCC) 4.8.0 doesn't treat the *Integer<double>()* as a constant expression.

```
requires_integer2.cpp:10:27: error: integral expression 'Integer<double>()'
is not constant
requires_integer2.cpp:10:27: error:   trying to instantiate
'template<bool Condition, class T> using requires = typename std::enable_if::type'
```

6.3 Trailing Return Type

We can also write the function interface to look like:

```
template <typename T>
auto odd(T n)
   -> requires<Integer<T>(), T>
{ return n & 1; }
```

i.e. we can write a function which returns an integer as

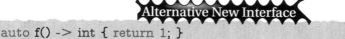

```
int f() { return 1; }
```

```
auto f() -> int { return 1; }
```

So, the above syntax helps us defer the explicit name of the return type with the blend of *auto* and deduction of the actual return type based on the type of the expression followed by ->.

This is known as *trailing-return-types*, which are sometimes very convenient when the return type of the function is a little complex.

Typically a *trailing-return-type* is most useful for a return type that would be overly complicated to specify before the function(*declarator-id*).

trailing-return-type:
    -> trailing-type-specifier-seq abstract-declarator$_{opt}$

6.3.1 Complex Return Type

Suppose, we want to write a function template, which will add 2 arguments of different types. Now, how to capture the type of the return type upfront as the interface of this function template.

An attempt may look like:

Ugly Interface

```
template <typename T, typename U>
decltype((*(T*)0) + (*(U*)0))
add(T t, U u);
```

With the help of *trailing-return-type*, we can simply write the clean interface as :

Cool Interface

```
template <typename T, typename U>
auto add(T t, U u) -> decltype(t + u);
```

6.3.2 auto type specifier

auto is a *type-specifier*, which denotes that

- ☞ the type of a variable being declared should be deduced from its initializer, or

- ☞ a function declarator should include a *trailing-return-type*.

As another example, let us write an interface for a function, which takes an argument of *double* and returns a pointer to a function taking an integer and returning a float:

representing complex return type was no simpler than this

```
// cool return type
auto f(double)->float(*)(int);
```

6.4 SFINAE Revisited

6.4.1 Return Type Based

Let us revisit the interface of the function *odd*:

SFINAE : Return Type Based

```
template <typename T>
auto odd(T n)
   -> requires<Integer<T>(), T>
{ return n & 1; }
```

6.4.2 Template Parameter Based

We can re-write the above based on template parameter based *sfinae* as:

SFINAE : Template Parameter Based

```
template <typename T, typename = requires<Integer<T>(), T>>
bool odd(T n)
{ return n & 1; }
```

6.5 IndirectlyCopyable

Now we are on a comfortable page with the *requires* as a powerful enabler towards the first step in designing the concept-based interface of the C++11 algorithm *copy_backward*:

Concept-Based Interface

```
template<BidirectionalIterator I, BidirectionalIterator Out>
requires IndirectlyCopyable<I, Out>
Out copy_backward(I first, I last, Out result);
```

As a second milestone, we have to reach towards the concept ***Indirectly-Copyable***.

IndirectlyCopyable concept requires that we can copy the value of an **I** iterator to an **Out** iterator.

It is not that difficult to infer that this concept is an alias for
Writable<ValueType<I>, Out>. So we h ave

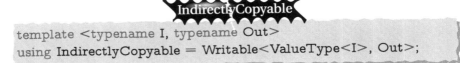

```
template <typename I, typename Out>
using IndirectlyCopyable = Writable<ValueType<I>, Out>;
```

Now, it's time to turn the leaf to build type functions to understand the concepts *ValueType* and *Writable* in the next chapter.

6.6 Source Code Listing

simulation of requires

```
1 #include <type_traits>
2
3 template <bool Condition, typename T = void>
4 using requires = typename std::enable_if<Condition, T>::type;
```
ch6/require.hpp

Listing 6.6.1: simulation of requires

basic example of sfinae on return type

```
1 int f(int i) { return i; }
2
3 template <typename T>
4 typename T::type f(T i) { return i; }
5
6 int main()
7 {
8    f(5);
9 }
```
ch6/basic_sfinae.cpp

Listing 6.6.2: basic example of sfinae on return type

```
   naive code without sfinae
1 #include <iostream>
2 #include <iomanip>
3
4 template <typename T>
5 bool odd(T n) { return n & 1; }
6
7 int main()
8 {
9    std::cout << std::boolalpha;
10
11   std::cout << odd(1) << std::endl;
12   std::cout << odd(2) << std::endl;
13   std::cout << odd(1.2) << std::endl;
14 }
                        ch6/requires_integer1.cpp
```

Listing 6.6.3:   naive code without sfinae

Integer trait

```cpp
1  #include <iostream>
2  #include "require.hpp"
3  #include <iomanip>
4
5  template <typename T>
6  constexpr bool Integer() { return std::is_integral<T>::value; }
7
8
9  template <typename T>
10 requires<Integer<T>(), T> odd(T n) { return n & 1; }
11
12 int main()
13 {
14    std::cout << std::boolalpha;
15
16    std::cout << odd(1) << std::endl;
17    std::cout << odd(2) << std::endl;
18    std::cout << odd(1.2) << std::endl;
19 }
```

ch6/requires_integer2.cpp

Listing 6.6.4: sfinae bound meta-function

Revisiting Interface

```cpp
1  int f() { return 1; }
2  auto f() -> int { return 1; }
```

ch6/new_function.cpp

Listing 6.6.5: Revisiting Interface

Without Trailing Return Type

```
1 template <typename T, typename U>
2 decltype((*(T*)0) + (*(U*)0))
3 add(T t, U u);
```

ch6/trailing_return_type1.hpp

Listing 6.6.6: Without Trailing Return Type

With Trailing Return Type

```
1 template <typename T, typename U>
2 auto add(T t, U u) -> decltype(t + u);
```

ch6/trailing_return_type2.hpp

Listing 6.6.7: With Trailing Return Type

Complex Return Type

```
1 // cool return type
2 auto f(double)->float(*)(int);
```

ch6/trailing_return_type3.hpp

Listing 6.6.8: Complex Return Type

```
     SFINAE : Return Type Based
 1  #include <iostream>
 2  #include "require.hpp"
 3  #include <iomanip>
 4
 5  template <typename T>
 6  constexpr bool Integer() { return std::is_integral<T>::value; }
 7
 8
 9  template <typename T>
10  auto odd(T n)
11      -> requires<Integer<T>(), T>
12  { return n & 1; }
13
14  int main()
15  {
16      std::cout << std::boolalpha;
17
18      std::cout << odd(1) << std::endl;
19      std::cout << odd(2) << std::endl;
20  }
                    ch6/requires_integer3.cpp
```

Listing 6.6.9:   SFINAE : Return Type Based

SFINAE : Template Parameter Based

```cpp
1  #include <iostream>
2  #include "require.hpp"
3  #include <iomanip>
4
5  template <typename T>
6  constexpr bool Integer() { return std::is_integral<T>::value; }
7
8
9  template <typename T, typename = requires<Integer<T>(), T>>
10 bool odd(T n)
11 { return n & 1; }
12
13 int main()
14 {
15    std::cout << std::boolalpha;
16
17    std::cout << odd(1) << std::endl;
18    std::cout << odd(2) << std::endl;
19 }
```

ch6/requires_integer4.cpp

Listing 6.6.10:   SFINAE : Template Parameter Based

Concept-Based Interface

```cpp
1  template<BidirectionalIterator I, BidirectionalIterator Out>
2  requires IndirectlyCopyable<I, Out>
3  Out copy_backward(I first, I last, Out result);
```

ch6/copy_backward_concepts.hpp

Listing 6.6.11:   Concept-Based Interface

```
1 template <typename I, typename Out>
2 using IndirectlyCopyable = Writable<ValueType<I>, Out>;
```

ch6/indirectly_copyable.hpp

Listing 6.6.12:   IndirectlyCopyable

Part III

Concept Design

Chapter 7

Type Functions

7.1 Value Type

Value Type of a given type *X* is type of the object of either of following two categories:

☛ that is being owned by X, or

☛ that is being referred by X.

So, value type of

☞ an array of integers is integer

☞ *vector<int>* is *int*

☞ *int** is *int*

Hence, the value type of

☞ a container is the type of the elements it contains.

☞ an iterator is the type of the element it refers to.

7.1.1 iterator_traits

As far as value type associated with an iterator is concerned, we have been relying on *typename iterator_traits<I>::value_type* traditionally.

So as a start, we could have looked at *ValueType<T>* as a template alias of *typename iterator_traits<I>::value_type* which will refer to the value type associated with a *Readable* iterator.

And, the forthcoming changes could have witnessed the replacement of the usage of *typename iterator_traits<I>::value_type* at all the places within STL with this invented template alias.
It is not difficult to foresee that this special kind of usage of template aliases as a gentle replacement of type traits is more than a welcome towards the implied simplification of specification of both the requirements as well as signatures of algorithms.

But, we didn't want to jump to this at once because it doesn't address the case for non-iterators yet and even for iterators, it was just one step towards one of the possibilities.

So, we look at *ValueType* as an associated member type for both the container and iterator.

Let us paint this picture.

7.1.2   Managing Substitution Failure

We need to provide a small set of types and type functions to help us build a simple framework for managing substitution failure in lookup.

The first type in this framework is an empty class to help us mark the case of substitution failure:

```
returned by type traits to indicate substitution failure
struct substitution_fail { };
```

So, *substitution_fail* is a type to indicate that a look-up has failed.

7.1.3   Type Predicates

Now, let us build two type predicates to represent both the case of failure as well as success in look-up as far as substitution is concerned.

```
Returns true if T indicates a substitution failure
template <typename T>
constexpr bool substitution_failed()
{
    return std::is_same<T, substitution_fail>::value;
}
```

```
Returns true if T indicates a substitution success
template <typename T>
constexpr bool substitution_succeeded()
{
    return !std::is_same<T, substitution_fail>::value;
}
```

7.1.4   Associated Value Type

All we wanted was to utilize *SFINAE* to distinguish the case of having *value_type* as a member type versus not having it without any compiler error.

So the case of having a *value_type* may look like:

```
template <typename U>
static typename U::value_type has_value_type(const U&);
```

Let us overload the above function *has_value_type* to be invoked in case of not having a *value_type* as follows:

```
static substitution_fail has_value_type(...);
```

Now we need a place to invoke this function:

```
using type = decltype(has_value_type(std::declval<T>()));
```

7.1.5 Get Value Type

Putting the above pieces together, we get :

get value type

```
template <typename T>
struct get_value_type
{
private:
    template <typename U>
    static typename U::value_type has_value_type(const U&);

    static substitution_fail has_value_type(...);

public:
    using type = decltype(has_value_type(std::declval<T>()));
};
```

We can have a convenient template alias to hold the nested *type* of *get_value_type*:

associated value type

```
template <typename T>
using associated_value_type =
    typename get_value_type<T>::type;
```

7.1.6 Type Predicate

Let us wrap this with a handy type predicate, which is a meta-function returning bool:

has associated value type

```
template <typename T>
constexpr bool has_associated_value_type()
{
   return substitution_succeeded<associated_value_type<T>>();
}
```

7.1.7 Deduced Value Type

It looks like we are all set for the associated contained type. All we need a mechanism now to work with similar situation in case of iterators or iterator-like types.

What it means is: if T can be deferenced then value type is the result of that operation(dereference) without qualified by reference and/or const.

7.1.8 Dereferenceability

This is helpful to deduce the result of the expression *t, again using *sfinae*:

get type after dereferencing

```
template <typename X>
static auto dereference(X&& a) -> decltype(*a);
```

report failure otherwise

```
static substitution_fail dereference(...);
```

In a nutshell :

get dereference result

```
template <typename T>
struct get_dereference_result
{
private:
    template <typename X>
    static auto dereference(X&& a) -> decltype(*a);

    static substitution_fail dereference(...);
public:
    using type = decltype(dereference(std::declval<T>()));
};
```

Let us have a convenient template alias for result type of the expression *t:

template alias

```
template <typename T>
    using dereference_result
        = typename get_dereference_result<T>::type;
```

An iterator of a vector of integers can be dereferenced:

dereferenceable iterator

```
static_assert(
    !std::is_same
    <
        dereference_result<std::vector<int>::iterator>,
        substitution_fail
    >
    ::value, "");
```

Whereas it is meaningless to dereference an integer:

int cannot be dereferenced

```
static_assert(
   std::is_same
   <
      dereference_result<int>,
      substitution_fail
   >
   ::value, "");
```

And, a type predicate to test the deferenceability:

test whether it could be dereferenced

```
template <typename T>
constexpr bool has_dereference()
{
   return substitution_succeeded<dereference_result<T>>();
}
```

Usage of has_dereference

We can use this as follows:

iterator can be dereferenced

```
std::cout << std::boolalpha;
// it prints true
std::cout << has_dereference<std::vector<int>::iterator>()
          << std::endl;
```

It prints *true*

simple struct

```
struct A {};
```

pointer to something can be dereferenced

```
std::cout << has_dereference<int*>() << std::endl;
std::cout << has_dereference<A*>() << std::endl;
```

It prints :
true
true

int cannot be dereferenced

```
std::cout << has_dereference<int>() << std::endl;
```

It prints *false*

A cannot be dereferenced

```
std::cout << has_dereference<A>() << std::endl;
```

It prints *false*

7.1.9 Structural Type

Let us recall that *ValueType* is supposed to give an associated type with an iterator or range or container. We needed a more generic way to lift the abstraction represented by *ValueType*.

Let us name this abstraction as *StructuralType*.

The *StructuralType* of a cv-qualified or reference type is the underlying type of the cv-qualifiers or reference.

All it means is : it represents the structure of the object being constrained, so that we can apply this to get the underlying type *T*.

Hence, we can say that the template alias *ValueType* can be looked as equivalent to a *StructuralType* associated with a container and/or an iterator or range.

So, the cool implementation may look like :

Structural Type

```
template <typename T>
using structural_type =
  typename std::remove_cv<
    typename std::remove_reference<T>::type
  >::type;
```

As expected, we can use the above representation as follows:

Using Structural Type

```
static_assert(
std::is_same<structural_type<int>, int>::value, "");

static_assert(
std::is_same<structural_type<const int>, int>::value, "");

static_assert(
std::is_same<structural_type<const int&>, int>::value, "");

static_assert(
std::is_same<structural_type<int*>, int*>::value, "");

static_assert(
std::is_same<structural_type<int[10]>, int[10]>::value, "");

static_assert(
!std::is_same<structural_type<int[10]>, int[1]>::value, "");

static_assert(
std::is_same<structural_type<A>, A>::value, "");
```

7.1.10 Value Type Deduction Framework

A value type deduction framework comprises of a set of simplified traits and overloaded functions, which can be easily adapted to reach the deduction of an associated type.

Typically, we can formulate this kind of framework in two layers:

- ☛ A function can play the role of a deduction hook, which will impart deduction rules specific to an applicable concept. We can represent different sets of concepts using

    - ☞ overloading these functions
    - ☞ constraining these functions

- ☛ A type trait can look-up for a nested name. In case of no such name is found, it may delegate to the deduction hook.

Let set the deduction hook as follows:

```
substitution_fail deduce_value_type(...);
```

The deduction framework will first search for a nested name, and then delegate to the concept-specific rules.

All this means is: if T can be dereferenced then we can deduce the value type as a result of dereference operation, but without any reference and const-qualifiers.

Let us have a tag type to indicate the selection of a default value to support class template specialization:

```
struct default_t { };
```

And, after this all hue n cry, our deduction framework looks like as follows:

```
                    Value Type Deduction
template <typename T>
   auto deduce_value_type(default_t, const T&)
     -> requires
        <
           has_dereference<T>(),
           structural_type
           <
              dereference_result<T>
           >
        >;
```

Now, we are all set to deduce the value type associated with *T* by adopting either of 2 ways:

☞ look-up for an associated member type if one such exists, else

☞ default to the deduction overloads.

So, the primary template may look like:

```
                 boilerplate code for value type deduction
template<typename T,bool = has_associated_value_type<T>()>
struct get_deduced_value_type;
```

Let us partially specialize it in case of existence of an associated member type

```
                    has an associated member type
template <typename T>
struct get_deduced_value_type<T, true>
{
   using type = typename get_value_type<T>::type;
};
```

Then, partially specialize it to fall to default deduction magic in case of no such look up, i.e., no associated member type:

```
                  no associated member type
template <typename T>
struct get_deduced_value_type<T, false>
{
   using type
     =
     decltype(deduce_value_type(default_t{}, std::declval<T>()));
};
```

Now, it looks like all required abstractions are built up. All we need to do now is to have a template alias to wrap these.

7.1.11 ValueType Template Alias

To recall, the value type is the type of object being owned or referred to. The value type is never cv-qualified or a reference.

```
                        Value Type
template <typename T>
using ValueType = typename get_deduced_value_type<T>::type;
```

This alias refers to the value type associated with *T*. It can be used with objects of any concept defining the notion.

Let us have a handy type predicate to check whether a value type ia associated with T as:

```
            returns true is T has an associated value type
template <typename T>
constexpr bool Has_ValueType()
{
   return substitution_succeeded<ValueType<T>>();
}
```

Now, we can start using the type function **ValueType** in any legal way we could have imagined.

☞ **value type for a container**

convenient template alias

```
using V = std::vector<int>;
```

vector does have a value type

```
static_assert(Has_ValueType<V>(), "");
```

value type of vector<int> is int

```
static_assert(std::is_same<ValueType<V>, int>::value, "");
```

☞ **value type must see through references**

expose the underlying type within reference qualifier

```
static_assert(std::is_same<ValueType<V&>, int>::value, "");
static_assert(std::is_same<ValueType<V&&>, int>::value, "");
static_assert(std::is_same<ValueType<const V&>,int>::value,"");
```

☞ **report if the type has no value type**

no value type

```
static_assert(!Has_ValueType<substitution_fail>(), "");
```

☞ **Check the value type for pointers**

value type for pointers

```
static_assert(Has_ValueType<int*>(), "");
static_assert(std::is_same<ValueType<int*>, int>::value, "");
```

☞ **The value types are the same modulo cv-qualifiers**

reveal value type

```
static_assert(Has_ValueType<int const*>(), "");
static_assert(std::is_same<ValueType<int const*>,int>::value,"");
```

☞ **peeping inside iterators**

value type of iterator

```
static_assert(std::is_same<ValueType<V::iterator>,
                           int>::value, "");
static_assert(std::is_same<ValueType<V::const_iterator>,
                           int>::value, "");
```

☞ **value type as contained value type**

owned value type

```
struct A {};

struct B { typedef int value_type; };

int main()
{
    static_assert( ! Has_ValueType<A>(), "" );

    static_assert(std::is_same<ValueType<B>, int>::value, "");
}
```

7.2 Writable

The concept *Writable* is always associated with an iterator.
An iterator type, *I*, is Writable if it permits the assignment of values of type
T to its referenced objects.

All it means is that, the following expression must be valid:

```
*i = t;
```

where i has type I and t is an expression having type T.

As we could have inferred is : the type can be qualified with const, and/or reference. For example, it can be const T& or T&&.

We need to embed two concepts to fulfill our requirements of *Writable* concept :

☞ *deferenceability* of the iterator type I. Fortunately, we have already built it in the form of *deference_result*. This will help us formulate the constrained expression **i* and this completes an elegant representation of the left hand side.

☞ *assignability* to help us constrain the assignment operation of the result of the dereferenced expression.

7.2.1 Assignable

We need this trait to determine if a type T supports assignment to a value of type U. U is generally expected to be a compound type.

This trait can be used to check for copy and move assignment by using reference types.

A positive response when U is an rvalue reference does not mean that T defines an assignment operator that specifically takes an rvalue reference to U (i.e., U&&). A copying assignment operator (taking const U&) will also satisfy the requirements of rvalue assignment.

Luckily, we already have a relevant type trait in the form of *std::is_assignable* which could be used to build a type predicate as follows:

Assignable

```
template <typename T, typename U>
constexpr bool Assignable()
{
    return std::is_assignable<T, U>::value;
}
```

We could start understanding it by using it for two kind of types like
move_only and *copyable* as follows:

move_only

```
struct move_only
{
  move_only(move_only&& x) { }
  move_only& operator=(move_only&& x) { return *this; }

  move_only(const move_only& x) = delete;
  move_only& operator=(const move_only& x) = delete;
};
```

sample class foo

```
struct foo { };
```

copyable

```
struct copyable
{
  copyable(const copyable& x) { }
  copyable& operator=(const copyable& x) { return *this; }

  copyable(const foo& x) { }
  copyable& operator=(const foo& x) { return *this; }
};
```

assignable with move_only

```
static_assert(Assignable<move_only, move_only&&>(), "");
static_assert(!Assignable<move_only,const move_only&>(),"");
```

assignable with copyable

```
static_assert(Assignable<copyable, copyable&&>(), "");
static_assert(Assignable<copyable, const copyable&>(), "");
```

assignability of copyable with foo

```
static_assert(Assignable<copyable, foo&&>(), "");
static_assert(Assignable<copyable, const foo&>(), "");
```

Please note that the first argument to *Assignable* can also be given as an
lvalue reference with the same meaning, i.e.,

$$Assignable < T\&, U > () \iff Assignable < T, U > ()$$

i.e., the type predicate `Assignable` is parameterized with 2 parameters of
type T as the type of object being assigned to and U as the type of value
being assigned, and it returns true if and only if an object of type T can be
assigned a value of type U.

Now, let us weave the above two concepts together to build the concept
`Writable`.

Writable

```
template <typename I, typename T>
constexpr bool Writable()
{
    return Assignable<dereference_result<I>, T>();
};
```

This is so cool as a powerful type predicate. Let us start using it to understand it better.

int* is writable to int

```
static_assert(Writable<int*, int>(), "");
```

iterator to vector<int> is writable to int

```
using V1 = std::vector<int>;

static_assert(Writable<V1::iterator, int>(), "");
static_assert(!Writable<V1::const_iterator, int>(), "");
```

```
                    same for unique pointer
using V2 = std::vector<std::unique_ptr<int>>;

static_assert(Writable<V2::iterator,
            std::unique_ptr<int>&&>(), "");
static_assert(!Writable<V2::iterator,
            const std::unique_ptr<int>&>(), "'");
```

It returns true if and only if I satisfies the syntactic requirements of the Writable concept with respect to the value type T, where I is an iterator type and T the type of values being written through iterators of type I.

Please note that the type T can be a reference type (e.g., const T& or T&&).

This is useful for writing test for copy and move assignment through the iterator.

7.3   Source Code Listing

Managing Substitution

```cpp
1  #ifndef _SUBSTITUTION_FAIL_HPP_
2  #define _SUBSTITUTION_FAIL_HPP_
3
4  #include <type_traits>
5
6  struct substitution_fail { };
7
8  template <typename T>
9  constexpr bool substitution_failed()
10 {
11     return std::is_same<T, substitution_fail>::value;
12 }
13
14 template <typename T>
15 constexpr bool substitution_succeeded()
16 {
17     return !std::is_same<T, substitution_fail>::value;
18 }
19
20 #endif
```

ch7/substitution_fail.hpp

Listing 7.3.1:   Managing Substitutions

Associated Value Type

```cpp
#include "substitution_fail.hpp"

template <typename T>
struct get_value_type
{
private:
   template <typename U>
   static typename U::value_type has_value_type(const U&);

   static substitution_fail has_value_type(...);

public:
   using type = decltype(has_value_type(std::declval<T>()));
};

template <typename T>
using associated_value_type =
   typename get_value_type<T>::type;

template <typename T>
constexpr bool has_associated_value_type()
{
   return substitution_succeeded<associated_value_type<T>>();
}
```

ch7/get_value_type.hpp

Listing 7.3.2:   Associated Value Type

Dereferenceability

```cpp
#ifndef _DEDUCED_VALUE_TYPE_HPP_
#define _DEDUCED_VALUE_TYPE_HPP_

#include "substitution_fail.hpp"

template <typename T>
struct get_dereference_result
{
private:
    template <typename X>
    static auto dereference(X&& a) -> decltype(*a);

    static substitution_fail dereference(...);
public:
    using type = decltype(dereference(std::declval<T>()));
};

template <typename T>
    using dereference_result
        = typename get_dereference_result<T>::type;

template <typename T>
constexpr bool has_dereference()
{
    return substitution_succeeded<dereference_result<T>>();
}


substitution_fail deduce_value_type(...);

#endif
```

ch7/deduced_value_type.hpp

Listing 7.3.3:   Dereferenceability

Testing Dereferenceability

```cpp
#include "deduced_value_type.hpp"
#include <vector>

int main()
{
    static_assert(
        !std::is_same
        <
            dereference_result<std::vector<int>::iterator>,
            substitution_fail
        >
        ::value, "");

    static_assert(
        std::is_same
        <
            dereference_result<int>,
            substitution_fail
        >
        ::value, "");
}
```

ch7/dereference_result.cpp

Listing 7.3.4:   Testing Dereferenceability

Usage of has_dereference

```cpp
1  #include "deduced_value_type.hpp"
2  #include <iostream>
3  #include <vector>
4  #include <iomanip>
5
6  struct A {};
7
8  int main()
9  {
10    std::cout << std::boolalpha;
11    // it prints true
12    std::cout << has_dereference<std::vector<int>::iterator>()
13          << std::endl;
14    std::cout << has_dereference<int*>() << std::endl;
15    std::cout << has_dereference<A*>() << std::endl;
16
17    // it prints false
18    std::cout << has_dereference<int>() << std::endl;
19    std::cout << has_dereference<A>() << std::endl;
20  }
```

ch7/has_dereference.cpp

Listing 7.3.5:   Usage of has_dereference

```
     Structural Type
 1  #include <type_traits>
 2
 3  template <typename T>
 4  using structural_type =
 5    typename std::remove_cv<
 6      typename std::remove_reference<T>::type
 7    >::type;
 8
 9  struct A {};
10
11  int main()
12  {
13    static_assert(
14    std::is_same<structural_type<int>, int>::value, "");
15
16    static_assert(
17    std::is_same<structural_type<const int>, int>::value, "");
18
19    static_assert(
20    std::is_same<structural_type<const int&>, int>::value, "");
21
22    static_assert(
23    std::is_same<structural_type<int*>, int*>::value, "");
24
25    static_assert(
26    std::is_same<structural_type<int[10]>, int[10]>::value, "");
27
28    static_assert(
29    !std::is_same<structural_type<int[10]>, int[1]>::value, "");
30
31    static_assert(
32    std::is_same<structural_type<A>, A>::value, "");
33  }
```

ch7/structural_type.cpp

Listing 7.3.6:   Structural Type

Type Deduction Hook

```cpp
1  #ifndef _DEDUCED_VALUE_TYPE_HPP_
2  #define _DEDUCED_VALUE_TYPE_HPP_
3
4  #include "substitution_fail.hpp"
5
6  template <typename T>
7  struct get_dereference_result
8  {
9  private:
10     template <typename X>
11     static auto dereference(X&& a) -> decltype(*a);
12
13     static substitution_fail dereference(...);
14  public:
15     using type = decltype(dereference(std::declval<T>()));
16  };
17
18  template <typename T>
19     using dereference_result
20        = typename get_dereference_result<T>::type;
21
22  template <typename T>
23  constexpr bool has_dereference()
24  {
25     return substitution_succeeded<dereference_result<T>>();
26  }
27
28
29  substitution_fail deduce_value_type(...);
30
31  #endif
```

ch7/deduced_value_type.hpp

Listing 7.3.7:   Type Deduction Hook

Value Type Deduction Framework

```cpp
1  #ifndef _DEDUCED_VALUE_TYPE_EXT_HPP_
2  #define _DEDUCED_VALUE_TYPE_EXT_HPP_
3
4  #include "deduced_value_type.hpp"
5  #include "structural_type.hpp"
6  #include "require.hpp"
7  #include "default.hpp"
8
9  template <typename T>
10    auto deduce_value_type(default_t, const T&)
11      -> requires
12        <
13          has_dereference<T>(),
14          structural_type
15          <
16            dereference_result<T>
17          >
18        >;
19
20
21 template <typename T>
22 struct get_value_type
23 {
24 private:
25   template <typename U>
26   static typename U::value_type has_value_type(const U&);
27
28   static substitution_fail has_value_type(...);
29
30 public:
31   using type = decltype(has_value_type(std::declval<T>()));
32 };
33
34 template <typename T>
35 using associated_value_type =
36   typename get_value_type<T>::type;
```

ch7/deduced_value_type_ext.hpp

Value Type Deduction Framework

```cpp
38 template <typename T>
39 constexpr bool has_associated_value_type()
40 {
41    return substitution_succeeded<associated_value_type<T>>();
42 }
43
44
45 template<typename T,bool = has_associated_value_type<T>()>
46 struct get_deduced_value_type;
47
48 template <typename T>
49 struct get_deduced_value_type<T, true>
50 {
51   using type = typename get_value_type<T>::type;
52 };
53
54 template <typename T>
55 struct get_deduced_value_type<T, false>
56 {
57   using type
58   =
59   decltype(deduce_value_type(default_t{}, std::declval<T>()));
60 };
61
62 template <typename T>
63 using ValueType = typename get_deduced_value_type<T>::type;
64
65 template <typename T>
66 constexpr bool Has_ValueType()
67 {
68   return substitution_succeeded<ValueType<T>>();
69 }
70
71 #endif
```

ch7/deduced_value_type_ext.hpp

Listing 7.3.8:   Value Type Deduction Framework

Using Value Type Deduction Framework

```cpp
1  #include "deduced_value_type_ext.hpp"
2  #include <vector>
3
4  int main()
5  {
6      using V = std::vector<int>;
7
8      static_assert(Has_ValueType<V>(), "");
9      static_assert(std::is_same<ValueType<V>, int>::value, "");
10
11     static_assert(std::is_same<ValueType<V&>, int>::value, "");
12     static_assert(std::is_same<ValueType<V&&>, int>::value, "");
13     static_assert(std::is_same<ValueType<const V&>,int>::value,"");
14
15     static_assert(!Has_ValueType<substitution_fail>(), "");
16
17     static_assert(Has_ValueType<int*>(), "");
18     static_assert(std::is_same<ValueType<int*>, int>::value, "");
19
20     static_assert(Has_ValueType<int const*>(), "");
21     static_assert(std::is_same<ValueType<int const*>,int>::value,"");
22
23     static_assert(std::is_same<ValueType<V::iterator>,
24                       int>::value, "");
25     static_assert(std::is_same<ValueType<V::const_iterator>,
26                       int>::value, "");
27 }
```

ch7/deduced_value_type_ext.cpp

Listing 7.3.9:   Using Value Type Deduction Framework

Writable Concept

```
1 #include "deduced_value_type_ext.hpp"
2 #include "assignable.hpp"
3
4 template <typename I, typename T>
5 constexpr bool Writable()
6 {
7     return Assignable<dereference_result<I>, T>();
8 };
```

ch7/writable.hpp

Listing 7.3.10:   Writable Concept

Using Writable Concept

```cpp
#include "writable.hpp"
#include <vector>
#include <memory>

int main()
{
    static_assert(Writable<int*, int>(), "");

    using V1 = std::vector<int>;

    static_assert(Writable<V1::iterator, int>(), "");
    static_assert(!Writable<V1::const_iterator, int>(), "");

    using V2 = std::vector<std::unique_ptr<int>>;

    static_assert(Writable<V2::iterator,
                  std::unique_ptr<int>&&>(), "");
    static_assert(!Writable<V2::iterator,
```

ch7/writable.cpp

Listing 7.3.11:   Using Writable Concept

Assignable Concept

```cpp
#include <type_traits>

template <typename T, typename U>
constexpr bool Assignable()
{
    return std::is_assignable<T, U>::value;
}
```

ch7/assignable.hpp

Listing 7.3.12:   Assignable Concept

Using Assignable Concept

```cpp
1  #include "assignable.hpp"
2
3  struct foo { };
4
5  struct move_only
6  {
7    move_only(move_only&& x) { }
8    move_only& operator=(move_only&& x) { return *this; }
9
10   move_only(const move_only& x) = delete;
11   move_only& operator=(const move_only& x) = delete;
12 };
13
14 struct copyable
15 {
16   copyable(const copyable& x) { }
17   copyable& operator=(const copyable& x) { return *this; }
18
19   copyable(const foo& x) { }
20   copyable& operator=(const foo& x) { return *this; }
21 };
22
23 int main()
24 {
25   static_assert(Assignable<move_only, move_only&&>(), "");
26   static_assert(!Assignable<move_only,const move_only&>(),"");
27
28   static_assert(Assignable<copyable, copyable&&>(), "");
29   static_assert(Assignable<copyable, const copyable&>(), "");
30
31   static_assert(Assignable<copyable, foo&&>(), "");
32   static_assert(Assignable<copyable, const foo&>(), "");
33 }
```

ch7/assignable.cpp

Listing 7.3.13:   Using Assignable Concept

Chapter 8

Putting Together

IV

Legacy Codebase

178   **Chapter 9**
Legacy

8.1   Concept-Based Sound Interface

Let us recall what was the ultimate goal outset at the beginning of this journey in the name of a sound interface for the algorithm *copy_backward*:

Concept-Based Sound Interface

```
template<BidirectionalIterator I, BidirectionalIterator Out>
requires IndirectlyCopyable<I, Out>
Out copy_backward(I first, I last, Out result);
```

8.2 IndirectlyCopyable

And the the concept `IndirectlyCopyable` demands that we can copy the value of an iterator I to the iterator Out.

For an output iterator Out and an in iterator I, we can express their syntactic requirement as:

IndirectlyCopyable requires *out = *in

- ☞ The value type of the iterator X can be represented as `ValueType<X>`.

- ☞ Copyability of the above to the iterator Out can be expressed as $Writable < I, ValueType < Out >>$.

$$IndirectlyCopyable < I, Out > \iff Writable < I, ValueType < Out >>$$

Let us use the feature *constexpr* to get the proper abstraction as follows:

IndirectlyCopyable

```
template<typename I, typename Out>
constexpr bool IndirectlyCopyable()
{
    return Writable<I, ValueType<Out>>();
}
```

It was really very cool to put everything together !!

8.3 Usage of IndirectlyCopyable

Now, we can easily use this abstraction as follows:

Simple Usage

```
static_assert(IndirectlyCopyable<int*, int*>(), "");
```

Same is the case with iterators as well:

iterators

```
using V1 = std::vector<int>;

static_assert(IndirectlyCopyable<V1::iterator,
                                 V1::iterator>(), "");
static_assert(IndirectlyCopyable<V1::iterator,
                                 V1::const_iterator>(), "");
static_assert(IndirectlyCopyable<V1::iterator, int*>(), "");
```

As can be seen easily that the concept of `Writable` was a better abstraction than the concept of `Output Iterator`.

`Writable` is a binary concept, i.e., a concept with two parameters, that expresses a relationship between an iterator type and a value type.

☞ It is not an intrinsic property of the iterator itself

☞ The value type being written may be unrelated to the value type of the iterator if one exists at all.

This will help us adopt a cleaner approach towards the implementation of iterator-framework.

All we can say about Out is that we can indirectly copy the values in the range [first, last) into the output range, hence the concept `IndirectlyCopyable` results into a simple and elegant concept.

8.4   Source Code Listing

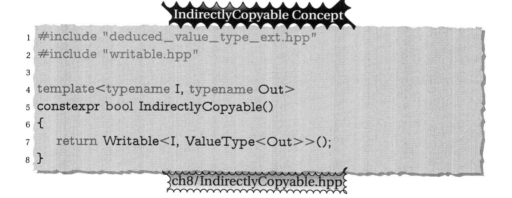

Concept-Based Sound Interface

```
1  template<BidirectionalIterator I, BidirectionalIterator Out>
2  requires IndirectlyCopyable<I, Out>
3  Out copy_backward(I first, I last, Out result);
```
ch8/copy_backward_concepts.hpp

Listing 8.4.1:   Concept-Based Sound Interface

IndirectlyCopyable Concept

```
1  #include "deduced_value_type_ext.hpp"
2  #include "writable.hpp"
3
4  template<typename I, typename Out>
5  constexpr bool IndirectlyCopyable()
6  {
7     return Writable<I, ValueType<Out>>();
8  }
```
ch8/IndirectlyCopyable.hpp

Listing 8.4.2:   IndirectlyCopyable Concept

Using IndirectlyCopyable Concept

```
1  #include "IndirectlyCopyable.hpp"
2  #include <vector>
3
4  int main()
5  {
6     static_assert(IndirectlyCopyable<int*, int*>(), "");
7
8     using V1 = std::vector<int>;
9
10    static_assert(IndirectlyCopyable<V1::iterator,
11                        V1::iterator>(), "");
12    static_assert(IndirectlyCopyable<V1::iterator,
13                        V1::const_iterator>(), "");
```

ch8/IndirectlyCopyable.cpp

Listing 8.4.3:   Using IndirectlyCopyable Concept

Writable Concept

```
1  #include "deduced_value_type_ext.hpp"
2  #include "assignable.hpp"
3
4  template <typename I, typename T>
5  constexpr bool Writable()
6  {
7     return Assignable<dereference_result<I>, T>();
8  };
```

ch7/writable.hpp

Listing 8.4.4:   Writable Concept

Type Deduction Hook

```cpp
1  #ifndef _DEDUCED_VALUE_TYPE_HPP_
2  #define _DEDUCED_VALUE_TYPE_HPP_
3
4  #include "substitution_fail.hpp"
5
6  template <typename T>
7  struct get_dereference_result
8  {
9  private:
10     template <typename X>
11     static auto dereference(X&& a) -> decltype(*a);
12
13     static substitution_fail dereference(...);
14  public:
15     using type = decltype(dereference(std::declval<T>()));
16  };
17
18  template <typename T>
19     using dereference_result
20         = typename get_dereference_result<T>::type;
21
22  template <typename T>
23  constexpr bool has_dereference()
24  {
25     return substitution_succeeded<dereference_result<T>>();
26  }
27
28
29  substitution_fail deduce_value_type(...);
30
31  #endif
```

ch7/deduced_value_type.hpp

Listing 8.4.5:   Type Deduction Hook

Value Type Deduction Framework

```
1  #ifndef _DEDUCED_VALUE_TYPE_EXT_HPP_
2  #define _DEDUCED_VALUE_TYPE_EXT_HPP_
3
4  #include "deduced_value_type.hpp"
5  #include "structural_type.hpp"
6  #include "require.hpp"
7  #include "default.hpp"
8
9  template <typename T>
10   auto deduce_value_type(default_t, const T&)
11     -> requires
12       <
13         has_dereference<T>(),
14         structural_type
15         <
16           dereference_result<T>
17         >
18       >;
19
20
21 template <typename T>
22 struct get_value_type
23 {
24 private:
25   template <typename U>
26   static typename U::value_type has_value_type(const U&);
27
28   static substitution_fail has_value_type(...);
29
30 public:
31   using type = decltype(has_value_type(std::declval<T>()));
32 };
33
34 template <typename T>
35 using associated_value_type =
36   typename get_value_type<T>::type;
```

ch7/deduced_value_type_ext.hpp

Value Type Deduction Framework

```cpp
38  template <typename T>
39  constexpr bool has_associated_value_type()
40  {
41      return substitution_succeeded<associated_value_type<T>>();
42  }
43
44
45  template<typename T,bool = has_associated_value_type<T>()>
46  struct get_deduced_value_type;
47
48  template <typename T>
49  struct get_deduced_value_type<T, true>
50  {
51      using type = typename get_value_type<T>::type;
52  };
53
54  template <typename T>
55  struct get_deduced_value_type<T, false>
56  {
57      using type
58      =
59      decltype(deduce_value_type(default_t{}, std::declval<T>()));
60  };
61
62  template <typename T>
63  using ValueType = typename get_deduced_value_type<T>::type;
64
65  template <typename T>
66  constexpr bool Has_ValueType()
67  {
68      return substitution_succeeded<ValueType<T>>();
69  }
70
71  #endif
```

ch7/deduced_value_type_ext.hpp

Listing 8.4.6:   Value Type Deduction Framework

Assignable Concept

```cpp
1  #include <type_traits>
2
3  template <typename T, typename U>
4  constexpr bool Assignable()
5  {
6      return std::is_assignable<T, U>::value;
7  }
```

ch7/assignable.hpp

Listing 8.4.7:   Assignable Concept

Managing Substitution

```cpp
1  #ifndef _SUBSTITUTION_FAIL_HPP_
2  #define _SUBSTITUTION_FAIL_HPP_
3
4  #include <type_traits>
5
6  struct substitution_fail { };
7
8  template <typename T>
9  constexpr bool substitution_failed()
10 {
11     return std::is_same<T, substitution_fail>::value;
12 }
13
14 template <typename T>
15 constexpr bool substitution_succeeded()
16 {
17     return !std::is_same<T, substitution_fail>::value;
18 }
19
20 #endif
```

ch7/substitution_fail.hpp

Listing 8.4.8: Managing Substitutions

Structural Type

```cpp
1  #include <type_traits>
2
3  template <typename T>
4  using structural_type =
5     typename std::remove_cv<
6        typename std::remove_reference<T>::type
7     >::type;
8
9  struct A {};
10
11 int main()
12 {
13    static_assert(
14    std::is_same<structural_type<int>, int>::value, "");
15
16    static_assert(
17    std::is_same<structural_type<const int>, int>::value, "");
18
19    static_assert(
20    std::is_same<structural_type<const int&>, int>::value, "");
21
22    static_assert(
23    std::is_same<structural_type<int*>, int*>::value, "");
24
25    static_assert(
26    std::is_same<structural_type<int[10]>, int[10]>::value, "");
27
28    static_assert(
29    !std::is_same<structural_type<int[10]>, int[1]>::value, "");
30
31    static_assert(
32    std::is_same<structural_type<A>, A>::value, "");
33 }
```

ch7/structural_type.cpp

Listing 8.4.9:   Structural Type

```cpp
1  #include <type_traits>
2
3  template <bool Condition, typename T = void>
4  using requires = typename std::enable_if<Condition, T>::type;
```

simulation of requires

ch6/require.hpp

Listing 8.4.10:   simulation of requires

Part IV

Legacy Codebase

Chapter 9

Legacy

*J*ust having a sound interface is not sufficient, though it can help us better in designing robust framework. But we already have a huge legacy in place on which we rely a lot, especially STL, Boost, Loki and similar highly peer reviewed libraries, it's high time to revisit this legacy codebase in practice in order to understand the impact of the sound interface.

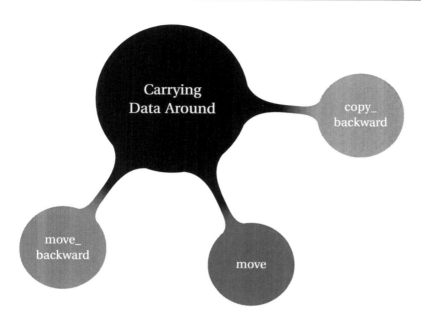

9.1 STL

9.1.1 Insertion into std::vector

interface

```
template <class _Allocator>
typename vector<bool, _Allocator>::iterator
vector<bool, _Allocator>::insert(const_iterator __position,
                        const value_type& __x)
{
  iterator __r;
```

if (size() < capacity())

capacity not exceeded

```
const_iterator __old_end = end();
++__size_;
_VSTD::copy_backward(__position, __old_end, end());
__r = __const_iterator_cast(__position);
```

if (size() > capacity())

create enough space

```
vector __v(__alloc());
__v.reserve(__recommend(__size_ + 1));
__v.__size_ = __size_ + 1;
```
create a temporary vector with size+1

copy

```
__r = _VSTD::copy(cbegin(), __position, __v.begin());
```
bring data upto position in the front of temporary vector

copy_backward

```
_VSTD::copy_backward(__position, cend(), __v.end());
```
bring data from position to the back of temporary vector

swapping the contents

```
swap(__v);
```

Finally assign the value x to the iterator r

```
    swap(__v);
```

Finally, the whole code looks like :

insertion into vector

```
template <class _Allocator>
typename vector<bool, _Allocator>::iterator
vector<bool, _Allocator>::insert(const_iterator __position,
                        const value_type& __x)
{
    iterator __r;
    if (size() < capacity())
    {
        const_iterator __old_end = end();
        ++__size_;
        _VSTD::copy_backward(__position, __old_end, end());
        __r = __const_iterator_cast(__position);
    }
    else
    {
        vector __v(__alloc());
        __v.reserve(__recommend(__size_ + 1));
        __v.__size_ = __size_ + 1;
        __r = _VSTD::copy(cbegin(), __position, __v.begin());
        _VSTD::copy_backward(__position, cend(), __v.end());
        swap(__v);
    }
    *__r = __x;
    return __r;
}
```

Let us look at another interface (overloaded one):

insertion

```
template <class _Allocator>
typename vector<bool, _Allocator>::iterator
vector<bool, _Allocator>::insert
(const_iterator __position,size_type __n,const value_type& __x)
{
    iterator __r;
    size_type __c = capacity();
    if (__n <= __c && size() <= __c - __n)
    {
        const_iterator __old_end = end();
        __size_ += __n;
        _VSTD::copy_backward(__position, __old_end, end());
        __r = __const_iterator_cast(__position);
    }
    else
    {
        vector __v(__alloc());
        __v.reserve(__recommend(__size_ + __n));
        __v.__size_ = __size_ + __n;
        __r = _VSTD::copy(cbegin(), __position, __v.begin());
        _VSTD::copy_backward(__position, cend(), __v.end());
        swap(__v);
    }
    _VSTD::fill_n(__r, __n, __x);
    return __r;
```

9.2 BOOST

Now, let us reveal the usage of the algorithm copy_backward within boost libraries. This will help us grab a chance to witness the power capabilities of a simple looking algorithm in multifaceted scenarios.

9.2.1 Compressed Sparse Row Graph

This is a special graph class which utilizes a CSR (Compressed Sparse Row) format to store directed and bidirectional graphs. This is useful for immutable data in high performance scenarios.

The CSR format stores vertices and edges in separate arrays, with the indices into these arrays corresponding to the identifier for the vertex or edge, respectively. The edge array is sorted by the source of each edge, but contains only the targets for the edges. The vertex array stores offsets into the edge array, providing the offset of the first edge outgoing from each vertex.

To achieve the above, it has two helper structures:

☞ `compressed_sparse_row_structure`

☞ `indexed_edge_properties`

Vertex and EdgeIndex are unsigned integral types

```
template <typename EdgeProperty,
  typename Vertex = std::size_t, typename EdgeIndex = Vertex>
class compressed_sparse_row_structure :
  public detail::indexed_edge_properties<
         compressed_sparse_row_structure<
             EdgeProperty, Vertex, EdgeIndex>,
         EdgeProperty,
         csr_edge_descriptor<Vertex, EdgeIndex>,
         csr_edge_index_map<Vertex, EdgeIndex> > {
```

The class `compressed_sparse_row_structure` maintains a collection of `Vertex` and `EdgeIndex`:

column and row descriptors

```
std::vector<EdgeIndex> m_rowstart;
std::vector<Vertex> m_column;
```

It has a member function template `add_edges_sorted_internal` to add edges from a sorted (smallest sources first) range of pairs and edge properties:

add sorted edges

```
template <typename BidirectionalIteratorOrig,
         typename EPIterOrig,
         typename GlobalToLocal>
void
add_edges_sorted_internal(
    BidirectionalIteratorOrig first_sorted,
    BidirectionalIteratorOrig last_sorted,
    EPIterOrig ep_iter_sorted,
    const GlobalToLocal& global_to_local) {
```

old and new rowstarts

```
edge_num old_rowstart = m_rowstart[i];
edge_num new_rowstart = m_rowstart[i] +
                        edges_added_before_i;
```

Now, it has to move old edges forward by the number of new edges before the counter i to make room. And, because new rowstart is greater than old rowstart, so it is advisable to use *copy_backward*:

old and new rowstarts

```
if (old_rowstart != new_rowstart) {
    std::copy_backward(m_column.begin() + old_rowstart,
            m_column.begin() + old_rowstart + old_degree,
            m_column.begin() + new_rowstart + old_degree);
    inherited_edge_properties::move_range
    (old_rowstart, old_rowstart + old_degree, new_rowstart);
}
```

Then it again needs *copy_backward* to move the range of old rowstarts to new rowstart backwards:

```
      inherited_edge_properties::move_range
      (old_rowstart, old_rowstart + old_degree, new_rowstart);
```

The class `indexed_edge_properties` maintains a collection of edge property

edge properties

```
public: // should be private, but friend templates not portable
```

It has a member function *move_range*, which helps move a specified range of properties backwards:

move backwards

```
void move_range(std::size_t src_begin, std::size_t src_end,
              std::size_t dest_begin)
{
  std::copy_backward(
     m_edge_properties.begin() + src_begin,
     m_edge_properties.begin() + src_end,
     m_edge_properties.begin() + dest_begin +
              (src_end - src_begin));
}
```

9.2.2 Interprocess Message Queue

This class allows sending messages between processes and allows blocking, non-blocking and timed sending and receiving.
It maintains a structure for message header

```
template<class VoidPointer>
class mq_hdr_t
  : public ipcdetail::priority_functor<VoidPointer>
```

Message Header

```
typedef typename boost::intrusive::
pointer_traits<void_pointer>::template
  rebind_pointer<msg_hdr_ptr_t>::type msg_hdr_ptr_ptr_t;
```

Pointer to the index

```
//Pointer to the index
```

Then it has a mechanism to check the segments for moving back or forward, followed by:

First Segment

```
if(!unique_segment){
std::copy_backward( &mp_index[0] + second_segment_beg
              , &mp_index[0] + second_segment_end
              , &mp_index[0] + second_segment_end + 1);
    mp_index[0] = mp_index[m_max_num_msg-1];
}
std::copy_backward( &mp_index[0] + first_segment_beg
              , &mp_index[0] + first_segment_end
              , &mp_index[0] + first_segment_end + 1);
```

insertion

```
msg_header & insert_at(iterator pos)
{
   const msg_hdr_ptr_t backup = *inserted_ptr_end();
   std::copy_backward(pos, inserted_ptr_end(),
                   inserted_ptr_end()+1);
   *pos = backup;
   ++m_cur_num_msg;
   return **pos;
}
```

9.2.3 Nesting STL Algorithm Invocations in lambda bind expressions

In order to use STL algorithms as target functions in lambda bind expressions, boost lambda library (BLL) defined these as function objects in the namespace `boost::lambda::ll`

copy_backward as struct

```
struct copy_backward {
```

It has a inner struct to represent a type capable of holding the number and type of the arguments:

argument pack

```
template <class Args>
struct sig {
  typedef typename boost::remove_const<
      typename boost::tuples::element<3, Args>::type
   >::type type;
};
```

Now comes the main part in the form of overloaded function call operator template to call the corresponding function templates of STL algorithms:

delegate to STL algorithm

```
template <class A, class C>
C
operator()(A a, A b, C c) const
{ return ::std::copy_backward(a, b, c); }

};
```

Let us have a 2D int array:

```
int a[2][4] = { {1,2,3,4},
                {10,20,30,40} };
```

Let us try printing the array using ranged-based for loop in a nested way:

```
for(auto row : a)
    for(auto col : row)
        std::cout << col << " ";
```

With clang 3.3, we got the error:

```
boost_bll_copy_backward_auto.cpp:9:22: error: invalid range expression of type
    'int *'; no viable 'begin' function available
    for(auto col : row)
                 ^ ~~~
1 error generated.
```

With gcc 4.8, the error is:

```
boost_bll_copy_backward_auto.cpp: In function 'int main()':
boost_bll_copy_backward_auto.cpp:9:24: error: no matching function for call to
 'begin(int*&)'
        for(auto col : row)
                 ^
```

With BOOST_FOREACH:

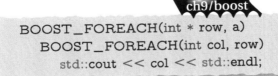

```
BOOST_FOREACH(int * row, a)
    BOOST_FOREACH(int col, row)
        std::cout << col << std::endl;
```

The error was:

```
error:
    no type named 'reference' in 'boost::detail::iterator_traits<int>'
    typedef typename boost::detail::iterator_traits<Iterator>::reference type;
                     ~~~~~^~
...
boost_bll_copy_backward_for_each.cpp:10:9: error: no matching function
for call
    to 'deref'
      BOOST_FOREACH(int col, row)
      ^~~~~~~~~~~~~~~~~~~~~~~~~~~
```

The above errors are clearly understood in the context of printing 2D array with array transcending to int* for subsequent dimension and there is no portable way to traverse on this with the help of begin/end/size artifacts.

So, we were back to :

simple printing

```
for(int row = 0; row < 2; ++row)
    for(int col = 0; col < 4; ++col)
        std::cout << a[row][col] << " ";
```

This prints: 1 2 3 4 10 20 30 40. Now, let us try using boost::lambda::ll::copy_backward:

simple usage

```
std::for_each(a, a + 2,
        bind(ll::copy_backward(), _1, _1 + 2, _1 + 4));
```

This prints: 1 2 1 2 10 20 10 20 as expected.

```
#include <boost/lambda/lambda.hpp>
#include <boost/lambda/bind.hpp>
#include <boost/lambda/algorithm.hpp>
#include <boost/foreach.hpp>

#include <iostream>

int main()
{
    using namespace boost::lambda;

    int a[2][4] = { {1,2,3,4},
                    {10,20,30,40} };

    for(int row = 0; row < 2; ++row)
        for(int col = 0; col < 4; ++col)
            std::cout << a[row][col] << " ";

    std::cout << std::endl;

    std::for_each(a, a + 2,
            bind(ll::copy_backward(), _1, _1 + 2, _1 + 4));

    for(int row = 0; row < 2; ++row)
        for(int col = 0; col < 4; ++col)
            std::cout << a[row][col] << " ";
}
```

9.2.4 Phoenix Adaptable STL Algorithms

Algorithm module in boost::phoenix provides wrapper over STL algorithms to make them callable with range as arguments where appropriate.
For example, with STL algorithm `copy_backward`, we need to provide iterators to both the start and end of the source vector as :

std::copy_backward

```
std::vector<int> v = {1, 2, 3};
std::list<int> l1(v.size()), l2(v.size());


std::copy_backward(v.begin(), v.end(), l1.end());
```

But, with phoenix algorithm module, we do not need to specify the start
and end of the source arguments. The analogous code using the phoenix
algorithm module is:

ch9/boost::phoenix::copy_backward

```
using boost::phoenix::copy_backward;
using boost::phoenix::arg_names::arg1;
using boost::phoenix::arg_names::arg2;


copy_backward(arg1, arg2)(v, l2.end());
```

testing

```
std::cout << std::boolalpha;
std::cout << std::equal(l1.begin(), l1.end(), l2.begin())
        << std::endl;
```

This prints : **true**

complete code

```
#include <boost/phoenix/core.hpp>
#include <boost/phoenix/stl/algorithm/transformation.hpp>

#include <iostream>
#include <iomanip>

int main()
{
    std::vector<int> v = {1, 2, 3};
    std::list<int> l1(v.size()), l2(v.size());

    std::copy_backward(v.begin(), v.end(), l1.end());

    using boost::phoenix::copy_backward;
    using boost::phoenix::arg_names::arg1;
    using boost::phoenix::arg_names::arg2;

    copy_backward(arg1, arg2)(v, l2.end());

    std::cout << std::boolalpha;
    std::cout << std::equal(l1.begin(), l1.end(), l2.begin())
            << std::endl;
}
```

A Little Inside Phoenix

The concept `Actor` models `Polymorphic Function Object` containing a valid Phoenix Expression, the evaluation of which gets started with a call to one of the overloaded function call operators.

First overload

```
template<class R, class I>
I operator()(R& r, I & i) const
{
    return std::copy_backward(detail::begin_(r),
                              detail::end_(r), i);
}
```

Second overload

```
template<class R, class I>
I const operator()(R& r, I const & i) const
{
    return std::copy_backward(detail::begin_(r),
                              detail::end_(r), i);
}
```

ch9/boost::phoenix::copy_backward

```
struct copy_backward
{
    template <typename Sig>
    struct result;

    template<typename This, class R, class I>
    struct result<This(R&, I)>
        : result<This(R&, I const &)>
    {};

    template<typename This, class R, class I>
    struct result<This(R&, I &)>
    {
        typedef I type;
    };

    template<class R, class I>
    I operator()(R& r, I & i) const
    {
        return std::copy_backward(detail::begin_(r),
                                  detail::end_(r), i);
    }

    template<class R, class I>
    I const operator()(R& r, I const & i) const
    {
        return std::copy_backward(detail::begin_(r),
                                  detail::end_(r), i);
    }
};
```

9.2.5 Spirit with Phoenix

It uses the library phoenix to attach semantic actions:

ch9/boost::phoenix::copy_backward

```
struct copy_backward
{
    template<class R, class I>
    struct result
    {
        typedef I type;
    };

    template<class R, class I>
    I operator()(R& r, I i) const
    {
        return std::copy_backward(detail::begin_(r),
                                  detail::end_(r), i);
    }
};
```

9.2.6   Range based version of copy_backward

ch9/boost::range::copy_backward

```
template< class BidirectionalRange,
          class BidirectionalTraversalWriteableIterator >
inline BidirectionalTraversalWriteableIterator
copy_backward(const BidirectionalRange& rng,
          BidirectionalTraversalWriteableIterator out)
{
    BOOST_RANGE_CONCEPT_ASSERT((
        BidirectionalRangeConcept<const BidirectionalRange> ));

    return std::copy_backward(boost::begin(rng),
                              boost::end(rng), out);
}
```

Usage

```
template< class Container >
void test_copy_backward_impl()
{
    Container source;
    typedef BOOST_DEDUCED_TYPENAME
    Container::value_type value_t;

    std::vector<value_t> target;
    target.resize(source.size());

    typedef BOOST_DEDUCED_TYPENAME
    range_iterator< std::vector<value_t> >::type iterator_t;

    iterator_t it=boost::copy_backward(source,target.begin());

    BOOST_CHECK( it == target.end() );
    BOOST_CHECK_EQUAL_COLLECTIONS(
        target.begin(), target.end(),
        source.rbegin(), source.rend() );

    BOOST_CHECK(
    it == boost::copy_backward(
    boost::make_iterator_range(source), target.begin()) );

    BOOST_CHECK_EQUAL_COLLECTIONS(
        target.begin(), target.end(),
        source.rbegin(), source.rend() );
}

void test_copy_backward()
{
    test_copy_backward_impl< std::vector<int> >();
    test_copy_backward_impl< std::list<int> >();
    test_copy_backward_impl< std::set<int> >();
    test_copy_backward_impl< std::multiset<int> >();
}
```

9.2.7   uBLAS : Basic Linear Algebra Library

Sparse Vector and Matrix

For implementing compressed version of a sparse vector, std::copy_backward is used internally, a glimpse of which can be seen below:

Element assignment

```
BOOST_UBLAS_INLINE
true_reference insert_element (size_type i, const_reference t) {
// duplicate element
   BOOST_UBLAS_CHECK (!find_element (i), bad_index ());
   if (filled_ >= capacity_)
      reserve (2 * capacity_, true);
   subiterator_type it(detail::lower_bound (index_data_.begin (),
                 index_data_.begin () + filled_, k_based (i),
                 std::less<size_type> ()));
   // ISSUE max_capacity limit due to difference_type
   typename
   std::iterator_traits<subiterator_type>::difference_type n
      = it - index_data_.begin ();
   BOOST_UBLAS_CHECK (filled_ == 0 ||
         filled_ == typename index_array_type::size_type (n) |
// duplicate found by lower_bound
               *it != k_based (i), internal_logic ());
   ++ filled_;
   it = index_data_.begin () + n;
   std::copy_backward (it, index_data_.begin () + filled_ - 1,
                 index_data_.begin () + filled_);
   *it = k_based (i);
   typename value_array_type::iterator
   itt (value_data_.begin () + n);
   std::copy_backward (itt, value_data_.begin () + filled_ - 1,
                 value_data_.begin () + filled_);
   *itt = t;
   storage_invariants ();
   return *itt;
}
```

Same is the case with sparse matrix as well.

Sparse Storage

```
Form Unique Associative Container concept
std::pair<iterator,bool> insert (const value_type &p) {
    iterator it = detail::lower_bound (
        begin (), end (), p, detail::less_pair<value_type> ());
    if (it != end () && it->first == p.first)
        return std::make_pair (it, false);
    difference_type n = it - begin ();
    resize (size () + 1);
    it = begin () + n;   // allow for invalidation
    std::copy_backward (it, end () - 1, end ());
    *it = p;
    return std::make_pair (it, true);
}
```

9.3   Source Code Listing

Concept-Based Sound Interface

```
1 template<BidirectionalIterator I, BidirectionalIterator Out>
2 requires IndirectlyCopyable<I, Out>
3 Out copy_backward(I first, I last, Out result);
```

ch8/copy_backward_concepts.hpp

Listing 9.3.1:   Concept-Based Sound Interface

Chapter 10

Closer Look

Evolution

$\mathcal{H}$aving studied the legacy usage of the algorithm
std::copy_backward, let us have an insider look into the legacy implementation approach of this algorithm by various schools to gain more understanding to help us build and extend the interface and implementation. This will definitely lay out the foundation with focus on adaptation
towards the evolution of C++11 and beyond.

10.1 libcxx

This framework keeps three overloaded function templates based on the
following categories of iterators:

- ☛ source is input iterator and target is output iterator.

- ☛ source and target satisfy certain criteria which is represented by the
  associated type traits. This is achieved by constraining the template
  parameters and the selection is determined by sfinae-based inclu-
  sion/exclusion function template overload.

- ☛ both the source and target are bidirectional iterators.

This helps us achieve certain performance-based optimizations as and
when possible. Let us have a closer look inside the implementation ahead.

10.1.1 Source is Input Iterator and Target is Output Iterator

input iterator to output iterator

```
template <class _InputIterator, class _OutputIterator>
inline _LIBCPP_INLINE_VISIBILITY
_OutputIterator
__copy_backward(_InputIterator __first, _InputIterator __last,
            _OutputIterator __result)
{
    while (__first != __last)
      *--__result = *--__last;
    return __result;
}
```

Its complexity is exactly (__last - __first) assignments, i.e., O(n), strictly linear.

But there are certain situations like : trivially copyable objects : where we could move blocks of memory using binary copy provided by memmove, keeping in mind that we want to support overlapping of source and target else we could have used memcpy. And the copy is always done in a non-destructive manner.

Fortunately, C++11 provides us with a type trait facility known as std::is_trivially_copy_assignable to capture this constraint-checking at compile time.

And we can use another type trait of C++11 : std::is_same to verify the equivalence of types of source and target types without any const-qualifier for the source.
 So, the algorithm may look like:

☞ compute the number of elements of source to be copied by utilizing pointer arithmetic, subtraction in this case. Say it is n. Time Complexity : O(1).

☞ shift the specified end of the target, i.e., result, by n in backward direction. Time Complexity : O(1).

☞ copy the n number of blocks, of size equal to either source or target, from the source to target. Time Complexity : O(n) (usually, but the constant can be very small)

Put together, the implementation is as follows:

10.1.2   sfinae based overload

```
template <class _Tp, class _Up>
inline _LIBCPP_INLINE_VISIBILITY
typename enable_if
<
    is_same<typename remove_const<_Tp>::type,_Up>::value&&
    is_trivially_copy_assignable<_Up>::value,
    _Up*
>::type
__copy_backward(_Tp* __first, _Tp* __last, _Up* __result)
{
    const size_t __n = static_cast<size_t>(__last - __first);
    __result -= __n;
    _VSTD::memmove(__result, __first, __n * sizeof(_Up));
    return __result;
}
```

So far good. But, we can have complex situations like:

☞ only source is trivially copyable

☞ only target is trivially copyable

☞ both source and target are trivially copyable

☞ source and/or target is move iterator. We will soon brief about what is move iterator.

☞ source and/or target are simple wrapper over iterators.

As we could see that we need at least one more interface to represent these combinations under a single roof.

But before we proceed, we need to find a mechanism to uncover the real type of iterators being passed.

unwrap_iter

This is a helper concept, manifested by the following function template overloads:

```plain
template <class _Iter>
inline _LIBCPP_INLINE_VISIBILITY
_Iter
__unwrap_iter(_Iter __i)
{
    return __i;
}
```

It is high time to brief about move iterators.

| **Move Iterators** :

Class template `move_iterator` is an iterator adaptor which provides its deference operation to implicitly convert the value of the underlying iterator deference operation to an `rvalue reference`. Rest of its behavior is intact with that of its underlying iterator.

In fact, we can use the same algorithms meant for copy-like semantics to be re-used wherever move-like version is intended. So there is no need to have a separate interface for move-like semantics as far as copy algorithms are concerned.

- replace_move

- replace_move_if

- remove_move

- remove_move_if

- unique_move

- reverse_move

- rotate_move

⁂ partition_move

⁂ partial_sort_move

⁂ move_if

⋮

We will talk about these scenarios in our forthcoming sequel : **Foundation of Algorithms in C++11, Volume 2** [1]

It is very useful to achieve copying with moving in case with move iterators.

simple example

```cpp
#include <list>
#include <vector>
#include <algorithm>

int main()
{
    std::list<std::string> l = {"abc", "defg", "hijkl"};

    // copies the contents of l to v1
    std::vector<std::string> v1(l.begin(), l.end());

    // moves the contents of l to v2
    std::vector<std::string> v2(std::make_move_iterator(l.begin()),
                        std::make_move_iterator(l.end()));
}
```

We can also call std::copy_backward with move iterators:

---

[1] Please visit our website www.algocoders.com for more details

simulating move_backward

```
#include <list>
#include <vector>
#include <algorithm>

int main()
{
    std::vector<int> v = {1, 2, 3};
    std::list<int> l;

    std::copy_backward(std::make_move_iterator(v.begin()),
```

All set with move iterators for now, we can proceed with our `unwrap_iter`:

sfinae with move_iterator

```
template <class _Tp>
inline _LIBCPP_INLINE_VISIBILITY
typename enable_if
<
    is_trivially_copy_assignable<_Tp>::value,
    _Tp*
>::type
__unwrap_iter(move_iterator<_Tp*> __i)
{
    return __i.base();
}
```

We can represent other wrapper over the underlying iterators as `wrap_iter`, which is a class template:

iterator wrapper

```
template <class _Iter>
class __wrap_iter
{
public:
   typedef _Iter iterator_type;

   typedef typename
   iterator_traits<iterator_type>::iterator_category
      iterator_category;

   typedef typename
   iterator_traits<iterator_type>::value_type
      value_type;

   typedef typename
   iterator_traits<iterator_type>::difference_type
      difference_type;

   typedef typename
   iterator_traits<iterator_type>::pointer
      pointer;

   typedef typename
   iterator_traits<iterator_type>::reference
      reference;

private:
   iterator_type __i;
```

All, we have to do is get the wrapped iterator by calling the member function base() on it:

```
                    sfinae with wrap_iter
template <class _Tp>
inline _LIBCPP_INLINE_VISIBILITY
typename enable_if
<
    is_trivially_copy_assignable<_Tp>::value,
    _Tp*
>::type
__unwrap_iter(__wrap_iter<_Tp*> __i)
{
    return __i.base();
}
```

Cool!

Now we can simply capture this status quo with another overloaded function template :

10.1.3 Both the source and target is bidirectional iterator

```
                    bidirectional iterators
template <class _BidirectionalIterator1,
          class _BidirectionalIterator2>
inline _LIBCPP_INLINE_VISIBILITY
_BidirectionalIterator2
copy_backward(_BidirectionalIterator1 __first,
              _BidirectionalIterator1 __last,
              _BidirectionalIterator2 __result)
{
    return _VSTD::__copy_backward(__unwrap_iter(__first),
                        __unwrap_iter(__last),
                        __unwrap_iter(__result));
}
```

10.2   libstdc++

This framework has a different constraining approach based on concept-checks, but still shares similarity towards the implementation of the algorithm `std::copy_backward`, where this inline function will try to utilize `memmove` as and when possible. Otherwise, it relies on certain compiler optimization techniques like loop unrolling in case of random access iterators because loop counter will be known.

It has concept checking embedded as a part of implementation of the algorithm rather than the interface.

10.3 Source Code Listing

```
1 template<BidirectionalIterator I, BidirectionalIterator Out>
2 requires IndirectlyCopyable<I, Out>
3 Out copy_backward(I first, I last, Out result);
```

Concept-Based Sound Interface

ch8/copy_backward_concepts.hpp

Listing 10.3.1:   Concept-Based Sound Interface

Part V

Evolution

Chapter 11

New Beginning

This book is just the tip of the iceberg as far as laying out basic foundation of C++11 algorithms is concerned. We have barely touched a tiny set of useful components, especially new ones and tried building concept-based framework to express the intent in the form of sound interface. Other important facets, like pre-conditions and post-conditions need to be addressed to build a broader range of compile-time framework.

The concepts listed and discussed in detail in the book : *Elements of Programming* is woven around *Writable*, *Readable* and *Regular* among commonly useful ones. Then it builds type attributes, type functions and properties. Among the techniques, the most applicable in the case of C++11 is : reduction to constrained sub-problem.

The ideas discussed in The Concept Design of STL revolves around the following concept diagrams:

213

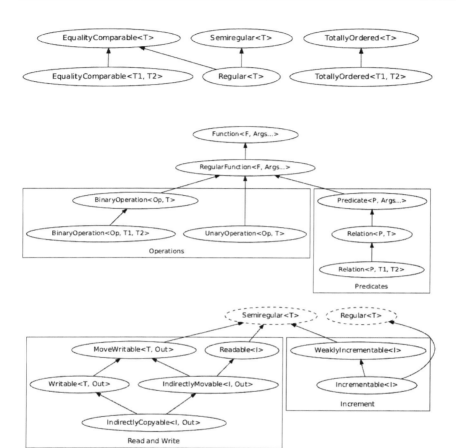

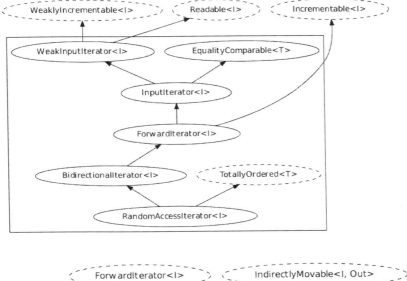

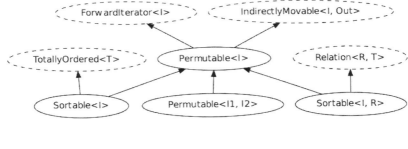

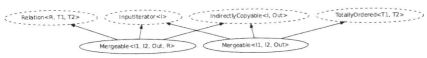

Its elegance is depicted by ease of emergence of cross-concepts along similar lines.

And the most challenging situation with these approaches is reliance on features of future C++, but it is simply not available today, or going to be available anytime soon.

11.1 Algocoders Approach

The uniqueness of our approach lies in strict and precise usage of C++11 features, both language and library ones, to help us understand the requirements of just one of the STL algorithms, namely, *std::copy_backward.*

We plan to take this journey to a new horizon by publishing our ideas, hitherto unknown to practicing software professional, in form of tiny booklets, comprising of 150-250 pages. This will help us concur both time and space without compromising with the rigor and turn-around time to bring these to limelight.

Index

Forthcoming Titles

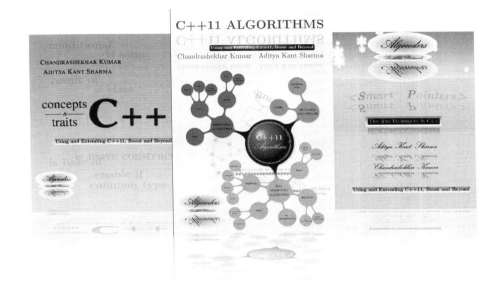

Printed in Great Britain
by Amazon.co.uk, Ltd.,
Marston Gate.